Burmese for Beginners

by
Gene Mesher
ဂျင်း မက်ရှာ

PAIBOON
PUBLISHING

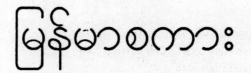
မြန်မာစကား

Burmese for Beginners
Copyright ©2006 by Gene Mesher

Printed in Thailand

Paiboon Poomsan Publishing
582 Amarinniwate Village 2
Nawamin 90, Bungkum
Bangkok 10230
THAILAND
Tel 662-509-8632
Fax 662-519-5437

orders@paiboonpublishing.com
www.paiboonpublishing.com

Paiboon Publishing
PMB 256, 1442A Walnut Street
Berkeley, California USA 94709
Tel. 1-510-848-7086, 1-800-837-2979
Fax 1-510-666-8862, 1-866-800-1840

Transliteration System: Gene Mesher and Benjawan Poomsan
Photos by the author

CD Voices: Gene Mesher, Pyu That Htar, Shwe Thway Maung, Pyu Wey Maung
and Min Soe Htwe

Cover photograph by Douglas Morton/Asia Pacific Media Services

ISBN 1-887521-51-8

Printed by Chulalongkorn University Printing House
Tel. 0-2218-3563   July 2009   [5209-251/1,500(2)]
http://www.cuprint.chula.ac.th

Table of Contents

Introduction

Welcome to the study of the language of Burma, officially known as Myanmar. Although about 50 million people live there, few books have been written to teach this language. This book, along with its accompanying CDs, attempts to fill that gap. It can be used for self-study, study with a tutor or as a classroom text.

Burmese is the largest member of the Tibeto-Burman language family of over 250 languages whose speakers live in the mountainous regions of the Himalayas east to the mountainous regions of southern China and northern Southeast Asia. Burmese has many features not found in Western languages such as the use of tones, including the verbs at the end of the sentence and the use of "bound" particles.

Burmese for Beginners teaches you four basic language skills: speaking, listening (using CDs), reading, and writing. Each lesson teaches new vocabulary, grammar and includes conversations and sentences to illustrate the materials presented in the book.

Each lesson also includes a section on how to read and write Burmese script. Learning the script is easier than it looks and will facilitate your understanding of Burmese. Although written Burmese doesn't use spaces between words, I have included them to help you master the script more easily. You'll also see that learning the Burmese alphabet is worth the trouble since it will help you better understand and pronounce the language.

The last section of the book includes two appendicies. The first appendix helps students plunge right into using the language: it lists many common phrases that students can use to make conversation or to use in their travels. The second gives the answers to the drills and quizzes that are set forth in each lesson. In order to facilitate review of the material presented in the book, the end section also includes a glossary of the words presented in the book, plus an index of grammar and reading/writing concepts presented throughout the book.

Although this book is written for beginners, it can also be used for those who want to improve their basic skills in Burmese, build a foundation for future studies or for those preparing to go on a trip to Myanmar.

Acknowledgements

First and foremost, thanks go to Paiboon's President, Benjawan Poomsan who has played a critical role in encouraging and steadfastly supporting this project as well as lending her strong background in Southeast Asian languages and publishing to ensure its success.

Grateful thanks also go to the many native Burmese speakers in Thailand and during my many trips to Myanmar especially Win Win Htwe, Deborah Aaron, Thet Thet Aung, Sabaey Aung, Aung Soe Min, Kay Maung La, Shwe Thway Maung, Pyu That Htar and Pyu Thein.

Thanks also to Nance Cunningham for her many excellent suggestions and reviews of drafts of the book. Her guidance and critical feedback has raised my knowledge of Burmese and this book to a much higher level.

To all of the above and others, I am truly thankful.

Gene Mesher
Bangkok,
November 2005

Guide to Pronunciation

Tones

Burmese has four tones listed below.

1. Creaky (.): a short and falling tone that ends with a weak closure of the glottis. Indicated by a subscript period. Often unmarked. Example: lạ က month

2. Low (no mark): a long and level that may fall or rise at the end. Example: la ကာ to come

3. High (:): a long tone that starts high, then falls slowly from high to low pitch. Example: la: ကာ: question particle (is it?)

4. Stopped ('): a very short, high tone ending in a glottal stop. Example: la' ကပ် middle

The Burmese tones can be shown schematically as follows:

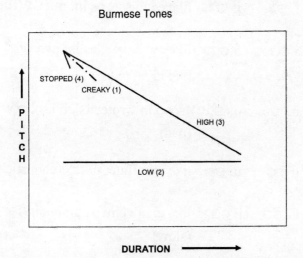

Burmese Tones

Vowels

Burmese vowels are best understood as a part of a vowel-tone-final consonant combination. Vowels can be thought of as belonging to one of three groups: open vowels (with no final consonant), final "n" vowels, and vowels with stopped finals. The vowels are listed below, and include the different forms the vowel may take, according to tone.

Open Vowels

/ə/   ə [အ]   like <u>a</u> in <u>a</u>bout; as in htə-min: ထမင်း (cooked rice)

/a/   ạ အာ့   a အာ   a: အား: like <u>a</u> in f<u>a</u>ther; as in: la လာ (come)

/e/   ẹ အဲ့   e အယ်   e: အဲ   like <u>e</u> in b<u>e</u>ll; be ဘယ် (which) [1]

/i/   ị အိ   i အီ   i: အီး: like <u>ee</u> in s<u>ee</u>; as in: mi: မီး (fire)

/ɔ/   ɔ့ အော့   ɔ အော်   ɔ:အော like <u>aw</u> in l<u>aw</u>; as in: pyɔ ပျော် (happy) [1]

/o/   ọ အို့   o အို   o: အိုး: like <u>o</u> in wr<u>o</u>te; as in: hso: ဆိုး: (bad)

/u/   ụ အု့   u အူ   u: အူး: like <u>u</u> in fl<u>u</u>te; tu တူ (chopsticks)

/ei/ ẹi အေ့   ei အေ   ei: အေး: like <u>ei</u> in v<u>ei</u>n: as in: hnei: နှေး: (slow)

---

[1] Note that the vowels e: and ɔ are special cases in which there is a high tone, but it is unmarked.

Final N Vowels

/an/ aṇ အန့် an အန် an: အန်း as in: pan: ပန်း (flower)

/in/ iṇ အင့် in အင် in: အင်း a short i, as in win ဝင် (enter)

/on/ oṇ အုန့် on အုန် on: အုန်း as in: yan-gon ရန်ကုန် (Rangoon)

/un/ uṇ အွန့် un အွန် un: အွန်း as in: zun: ဇွန်း (spoon)

/ain/ aiṇ အိုင့် ain အိုင် ain: အိုင်း as in: hsain ဆိုင် (store)

/ein/ eiṇ အိန့် ein အိန် ein: အိန်း as in: ein: အိမ် (house)

/aun/ auṇ အောင့် aun အောင် aun: အောင်း
                                          as in: kaun: ကောင်း (good)

Stopped Final Vowels (stopped tone only)

/a'/   အတ်၊ အပ်   as in hpa' ဖတ် (read)

/e'/   အက်   as in je' ကြက် (chicken)

/i'/   အစ်   as in hni' နှစ် (year)

/o'/   အုတ်၊ အုပ်   as in sa-o' စာအုပ် (book)

/u'/   အွတ်   as in lu'-la' လွတ်လပ် (independent)

/ai'/ အိုက်   as in lai' လိုက် (follow)

/ei'/ အိတ်၊ အိပ်   as in ə-yei' အရိပ် (shadow)

/au'/ အောက်   as in nau' နောက် (next)

Weakening

When two words are combined, Burmese vowels sometimes
become 'weakened'. That is, the original vowel sound is replaced
with a shwa (ə), such as the sound in the English words *a*bout and
*u*pon. Some common example of this in Burmese are:

ti' တစ်(one)   tə-hse တစ်ဆယ်(ten)   tə-ya တစ်ရာ(100)

hni' နှစ်(two)   hnə-hse နှစ်ဆယ်(twenty)   hnə-ya နှစ်ရာ(200)

A more detailed discussion of weakening is given in Lesson 7.

Consonants

/b/   ပ | ဘ   as in baby; be ဘယ် (left)

/d/   ဒ | ဓ   as in doll; da: ဓား (knife)

/dh/   သ   like the voiced th in this; pan:-dhi: ပန်းသီး (apple)

/g/   ဂ   as in gold, gi-ta̞ ဂီတ (music)

/h/   ဟ   as in honey; ho'-ke̞, ဟုတ်ကဲ့ (yes)

/j/   ကျ | ကြ   similar to ch in chin, but with no aspiration and

                   formed using the flat of the tongue (often

                   transliterated as ky or kj); ja: ကျား (tiger)

/ɉ/   ဂျ | ဂြ   as in English jaw, but formed using the flat of the

                   tongue (often transliterated as gy or gj); ɉə-pan

                   ဂျပန် (Japan)

/k/   က   as in skate (i.e., unaspirated); ka: ကား (car)

| /l/ | လ | as in law; lan: လမ်း (road) |

/l/ လ as in law; lan: လမ်း (road)

/m/ မ as in money; ma မာ (hard)

/n/ န as in need; na-yi, နာရီ (hour)

/ng/ င as in ringing; nga: ငါး (fish)

/ny/ ည like ñ in piñata; nya ညာ (right)

/p/ ပ as in pink; pai'-hsan ပိုက်ဆံ (money)

/r/ ရ as in red (used in loan words); re-di-yo ရေဒီယို (radio)

/s/ စ as in soup; sa-o' စာအုပ် (book)

/sh/ ရှ၊ လျှ as in shark; shi-de ရှိတယ် (to have)

/t/ တ same as the unaspirated t in standard; te' တတ် (be able to)

/th/ သ like the unvoiced th in thin; thon: သုံး (three)

/w/ ဝ like w in woman; win-de ဝင်တယ် (to enter)

/y/ ယ ၊ ရ as in you; yei ရေ (water)

/z/ ဇ ၊ ဈ as in English zebra; zei: ဈေး (market)

/'/ က်၊စ်၊တ်၊ပ် glottal stop as in lock, but w/o the puff of air at the end (final consonant only); we' ဝက် (pig)

Aspirated Consonants

Aspiration means the speaker breathes out heavily while making a
consonant sound. Burmese has many aspirated consonants. Some
are listed as separate letters in the Burmese alphabet. Other
aspirated consonants are written using ha̱-hto: (̱).

ch   ချ   same as English ch as in chew, but more aspirated
               (paired with ကျ); cha:-na: ခြားနား (different)

hk   ခ   like k̲ in k̲ill, but more aspirated (paired with က);
               hke' ခက် (difficult)

hl   လှ   like l but aspirated (no English equivalent); hla̱ လှ
               (pretty)

hm   မှ   like m but aspirated; -hma မှာ (at)

hn   နှ   like n but aspirated, hna နှာ (nose)

hng   ငှ   like ng but aspirated; hnge' ငှက် (bird)

hny   ညှ   like ny but aspirated; hnya' ညှပ် (cut)

hp   ဖ   as in English pore (paired with ပ); hpə-na' ဖိနပ် (shoe)

hs   ဆ   same as s but aspirated (paired with စ); hsei: ဆေး
               (medicine)

ht   ထ   as t in t̲ense but more aspirated (paired w/ တ); hti: ထီး
               (umbrella)

hw   ှွ   like w but aspirated; hwe' ှွက် (hide)

Note that the "sh" sound is also a special case that also uses hạ-hto: and is represented by either yạ-gau' hạ-hto: (ရှ) or lạ yạ-piṇ hạ-hto: (လျှ) depending on the word.

Medial Consonants

Special symbols are used to indicate medial "y" and "w" sounds. Two symbols are used for the 'y' sound: yạ-piṇ (ျ) and yạ-yi' (ြ). The medial w sound uses the wạ-hswe symbol (ွ). Examples are found in many words such as the verbs for want (ချိၓ chin), speak (ပြော pyɔ:) and go (သွာ: thwa:), respectively.

Final Consonants

Burmese has only two "syllable ending" consonants, the glottal stop and the nasal n. The glottal is similar to the beginning of the final k sound in the word lock but without the explosion that follows. The Burmese nasal "n", is like a shortened version of the English 'n' sound at the beginning of "un-hunh".

Glottal stops and nasal n's are formed by adding a "killer" mark (ə-tha', which looks like a superscript 'c') to one of four possible consonants. The glottal stops are: က် (kạ-tha'), စ် (sạ-tha'), တ် (tạ-tha') and ပ် (pạ-tha') and the nasal n's are: င် (ngạ-tha'), ည် (nyạ-tha'), န် (nạ-tha') and မ် (mạ-tha').

Voicing

As in English, some Burmese consonants may be "voiced", meaning that a humming sound is made in the voice box along with forming the consonant in the mouth (The English 'z' sound is an example.) The "voiceable" Burmese consonants are:

Unvoiced consonant	pronounced when voiced as:
j (ကျ), ch (ချ)	j̄ (ဂျ)
k (က), hk (ခ)	g (ဂ)
p (ပ), hp (ဖ)	b (ဘ)
s (စ), hs (ဆ)	z (ဇ)
t (တ), ht (ထ)	d (ဒ)
th (သ)	dh (ဿ)[2]

Note that initial consonants and those following a glottal stop are usually not voiced, but there are sometimes exceptions that are.

Common examples of voicing include the polite particle -pa (ပါ), voiced as "-ba". and the present/past verb suffix -te (တယ်), voiced as "-de". More than one syllable can be voiced at the same time. The Burmese word for "thank you", for example, includes the voiced forms of both "-pa" and "-te": jei:-zu: tin-**ba**-**de** ကျေးဇူး တင်ပါတယ်.

---

[2] The 'dh' sound is like the voiced form of <u>th</u> in the words '<u>th</u>is' and '<u>th</u>at', while the unvoiced form (transliterated as 'th') is like the <u>th</u> sound in <u>th</u>ing.

Similar Tone, Consonant and Vowel Sounds

A major obstacle in language learning is being able to hear and clearly say words with similar sounds. Some Burmese words have the same sound but different tones. In other cases, the difference is that one word has an aspirated consonant while the other does not. Some words also have different, but hard to distinguish consonants. Here are just a few of the many examples of similar sounding words.

Same sound, different tone

lạ	လ	month
la	လာ	to come
la:	လား	question particle (is it?)
la'	လတ်	middle
kạ	က	to dance, from (part.)
ka	ကာ	shield
ka:	ကား	car, automobile
ka'	ကတ်	card
sạ	စ	to start
sa	စာ	writing
sa:	စား	eat
sa'	စပ်	spicy
meị	မေ့	forget
mei	မေ	May
mei:	မေး	to ask
mei'	မိတ်	prickly heat

Unaspirated vs. aspirated consonants

sa :	စား	to eat	hsa:	ဆား	salt
la̰	လ	month	hla̰	လှ	pretty
ma	မာ	hard	hma	မှာ	at (part.)
jo	ကျို	boil	cho	ချို	sweet
nga:	ငါး	five	hnga:	ငှား	lend

Different, but similar consonants

kaun:	ကောင်း	good	gaun:	ခေါင်း	head
na	နာ	pain	nga	ငါ	I (informal)
nei	နေ့	live, stay	ne	နယ်	state (geog.)
ngo	ငို	cry	nyo	ညို	brown
be'	ဘက်	side	pei:	ပေး	give
mei:	မေး	ask	myei:	မြေး	grandchild
daun̰	ထောင့်	corner	taun	တောင်	south
hse	ဆယ်	ten	hsei:	ဆေး	medicine

The Burmese Alphabet

က
ka-ji:
ကကြီး

ခ
hka-gwe:
ခခွေး

ဂ
ga-nge
ဂငယ်

ဃ
ga-ji:
ဃကြီး

င
nga
င

စ
sa-lon:
စလုံး

ဆ
hsa-lein
ဆလိမ်

ဇ
za-gwe:
ဇကွဲ

ဈ
za-myin:-zwe:
ဈမျဉ်းဆွဲ

ည
nya
ည

ဍ
ta-ta-lin:-jei'
ဍသန်လျင်းချိတ်

ဎ
hta-win:-be:
ဎဝမ်းဘဲ

ဌ
da-yin-gau'
ဌရင်ကောက်

ဋ
da-yei-hmo'
ဋရေမှုတ်

ဏ
na-ji:
ဏကြီး

တ
ta-wun:-bu
တဝမ်းပူ

ထ
hta-hsin-du:
ထဆင်ထူး

ဒ
da-dwei:
ဒထွေး

ဓ
da-au'-chai'
ဓအောက်ခြိုက်

န
na-nge
နငယ်

ပ
pa-zau'
ပစောက်

ဖ
hpa-u:-hto'
ဖဦးထုပ်

ဗ
ba-da-chai'
ဗထက်ခြိုက်

ဘ
ba-gon:
ဘကုန်း

မ
ma
မ

ယ
ya-pe'-le'
ယပက်လက်

ရ
ya-gau'
ရကောက်

လ
la
လ

ဝ
wa
ဝ

သ
tha
သ

ဟ
ha
ဟ

ဠ
la-ji:
ဠကြီး

အ
a
အ

Vowel Symbols

ာ ါ   /a/   yei:-chạ (short & long form) ‌ရေးချ

◌ိ   /ị/   lon:-ji:-tin လုံးကြီးတင်

◌ီ   /i/   lon:-ji:-tin hsan-hka' လုံးကြီးတင် ဆန်ခတ်

ု | /ụ/   tə-chaun:-ngin တစ်ချောင်းငင်

ူ ‖   /u/   hnə-chaun:-ngin (short & long form) နှစ်ချောင်းငင်

ေ   /ei/   thə-wei-hto: သဝေထိုး

◌ဲ   /e:/[3]   nau'-pyi' နောက်ပစ်

ော   /ɔ:/[4]   thə-wei-hto: yei:-chạ သဝေထိုး ‌ရေးချ

ော်   /ɔ/   thə-wei-hto: yei:-chạ shẹi-hto: သဝေထိုး ‌ရေးချ ‌ရှေ့ထိုး

ောက်   /au'/   thə-wei-hto: yei:-chạ shẹi-hto: kạ-tha'...

                            သဝေထိုး ‌ရေးချ ‌ရှေ့ထိုး ကသတ်

ောင်   /aun/   thə-wei-hto: yei:-chạ shẹi-hto: ngạ-tha'...

                            သဝေထိုး ‌ရေးချ ‌ရှေ့ထိုး ငသတ်

◌ို   /o/   lon:-ji:-tin tə-chaun:-ngin လုံးကြီးတင် တစ်ချောင်းငင်

◌ိုက်   /ai/   lon:-ji:-tin tə-chaun:-ngin kạ-tha'...

                    လုံးကြီးတင် တစ်ချောင်းငင် ကသတ်

◌ိုင်   /ain/   lon:-ji:-tin tə-chaun:-ngin ngạ-tha'...

                    လုံးကြီးတင် တစ်ချောင်းငင် ငသတ်

---

[3] These two vowels include unmarked high tones.

Special and Clustered Consonant Symbols

ျ	ya̱-pin̊ ယပင့် medial 'y' sound
ြ/ြ	ya̱-yi' ရရစ် medial 'y' sound
ွ	wa̱-hswe: ဝဆွဲ medial 'w' sound
ှ	ha̱-hto: ဟထိုး indicates aspiration
ွျ	ya-pin wa̱-hswe: ယပင့် ဝဆွဲ combined symbol
ျှ	ya̱-pin̊ ha̱-hto: ယပင့် ဟထိုး combined symbol
ွှ	wa̱-hswe: ha̱-hto: ဝဆွဲ ဟထိုး combined symbol
ျွ	ha̱-hto: tə-chaun:-ngin ဟထိုး တစ်ချောင်းငင်

combined symbol

ျွ	ha̱-hto: hnə-chaun:-ngin ဟထိုး နှစ်ချောင်းငင်

combined symbol

Tone Marks and Final Consonant Symbols

း   :   wə-sạ-hnə-lon:-bau' ဝစ္စနှစ်လုံးပေါက် high tone mark

့   .   au'-kạ-myi' အောက်ကမြစ် indicates creaky tone (subscript period)

်   '   ə-tha' ("killer" stroke) အသတ် indicates final 'n' consonant if above င, ည, န or မ indicates final glottal stop if placed above က, စ, တ or ပ

်   sheị-hto: ရှေ့ထိုး same as ə-tha' when used with yei:-chạ (ါ). Does not indicate closed syllable

ံ   n   thei:-dhei:-tin သေးသေးတင် indicates a final "n" sound (marked with a superscript period)

Punctuation

Burmese uses just two punctuation marks, a short, vertical line: ၊ whose function is similar to a comma, and two short vertical lines: ။ used as an end of sentence marker:

။   po-mạ ပုဒ်မ (end of sentence marker)

၊   po-hti: ပုဒ်ထီး (comma)

Lesson 1

greetings; polite particles; negative sentences; final
question particles; numbers; consonants I;
simple vowels

thin-gan:-za ti'   သင်ခန်းစာ ၁   Lesson 1
wɔ:-ha-rạ   ဝေါဟာရ   Vocabulary

Nouns

jə-mạ	ကျွန်မ	I (female speaker)
jən-dɔ, jə-nɔ	ကျွန်တော်	I (male speaker)
hkə-mya:	ခင်ဗျား	you (male speaker)
hkə-mya:-dọ	ခင်ဗျားတို့	you (male speaker, plural)
shin	ရှင်	you (female speaker)
shin-dọ	ရှင်တို့	you (female speaker, plural)
thu	သူ	he, she or it
da, di	ဒါ၊ ဒီ	this
e:-da, e:-di	အဲဒါ၊ အဲဒီ	that
ho-ha	ဟိုဟာ	that one over there
na-me	နာမည်	name
ho'-kẹ	ဟုတ်ကဲ့	yes (lit., "that's right")
myei-bon	မြေပုံ	map
sa-o'	စာအုပ်	book
thə-din:-za	သတင်းစာ	newspaper
na-yi	နာရီ	watch, clock, hour
bɔ:-pin	ဘောပင်	pen
hke:-dan	ခဲတံ	pencil
ei'	အိတ်	bag
ba	ဘာ	what?
da-ba-le:	ဒါဘာလဲ	"What is this?"
mə-ho'-hpu:	မဟုတ်ဘူး	not so/ no, ("that's not right")
ho'-kẹ-ba	ဟုတ်ကဲ့ပါ။	"Yes, Sir!"

Verbs

na:-le-de	နားလည်တယ်	to understand, "[I] understand."
na:-le-yẹ-la:	နားလည်ရဲ့လား။	"Do you understand?"
na:-mə-le-bu:	နားမလည်ဘူး။	"[I] don't understand."
hkɔ-de	ခေါ်တယ်	to be called
yạ-de	ရတယ်	to get, obtain, have
yạ-ba-de	ရပါတယ်	"That's all right."
yạ-mə-la:?	ရမလား	"May I... (do something)?"
zei:-cho-de	ဈေးချိုတယ်	to be cheap, inexpensive

Particles

-pa/ba	ပါ	polite particle
-te/de	တယ်	present/past verb particle
-la:?	လား	'Yes/No question' particle
-le:?	လဲ	'open question' particle
-nɔ?	နော်	informal final part. ("...right?")
-le:	လည်း	too, also
-gɔ:	ကော	noun part. emphasizes person being spoken to ("and you?")
-lau'	လောက်	noun particle for about (as in "about how much?")

Other Useful Phrases

nei-kaun:-ye̱-la:	နေကောင်းရဲ့လား	"How are you doing?"
nei-kaun:-ba-de	နကောင်းပါတယ်	"[I'm] Fine."
twei̱-ya̱-da wun:-tha-ba-de	တွေ့ရတာ ဝမ်းသာပါတယ်။	"Nice to meet you."
hsɔ:-ri:-nɔ?	ဆောရီးနော်။	"I'm sorry."
kei'-sa̱-mə-shi̱-bu:	ကိစ္စမရှိဘူး။	"It doesn't matter." "No problem."
jei:-zu:-tin-ba-de	ကျေးဇူးတင်ပါတယ်။	"Thank you."
jei:-zu:-be:	ကျေးဇူးပဲ။	"Thanks."
da be-lo hkɔ-dhə-le:	ဒါ ဘယ်လို ခေါ်သလဲ။	"What is this called?"
na-me be-lo hkɔ-dhə-le:	နာမည် ဘယ်လို ခေါ်သလဲ။	"What's your name?"
be-lau'-le:	ဘယ်လောက်လဲ။	"How much [is that]?"
yu-me	ယူမယ်။	"[I'll] take it" (said when buying something).
di-hma pai'-hsan	ဒီမှာ ပိုက်ဆံ။	"Here's the money" (said when paying a bill).

thə-da   သဒ္ဒါ   **Grammar**

Greetings

Min-gə-la-ba မင်္ဂလာပါ, meaning "auspiciousness", is used as a
greeting used between teachers and students, it is also used by
Burmese to greet foreigners, but not in every day conversation
between Burmese speakers. Instead, a variety of phrases are used
under different circumstances. The most common are:

nei-kaun-yẹ-la?	နေကောင်းရဲ့လား။	How are you?
sa:-pi:-bi-la:?	စားပြီးပြီလား။	Have you eaten yet?
be thwa:-mə-le:	ဘယ် သွားမလဲ။	Where are you going?
be-gạ pyan-la-le:?	ဘယ်က ပြန်လာလဲ။	Where did you go?

Instead of "goodbye", Burmese use the phrase:
thwa:-bi   သွားပြီ။   I am going.

Being Polite: shin/hkə-mya.

A special word is used to politely address the person one is
speaking to. The word for males is hkə-mya: (ခင်ဗျား) while
female speakers use the word shin (ရှင်). The conversations and
sentences include many examples of this.

Being Polite: the 'pa/ba' particle

The other way to make a statement more polite is to use the "pa/ba" particle (written "pa" but voiced as "ba"), which is usually placed after the verb. For example:

I don't understand.	na:-mə-le-bu:	နားမလည်ဘူး။
Can also be written:	na-mə-le-**ba**-bu:	နားမလည်ပါဘူး။

The -pa/ba particle is used when the speaker wishes to be polite and is often used when speaking to someone respectfully, such as with the elderly, monks and teachers.

Final question particles: la: လား and le: လဲ

Questions in Burmese usually include a special question particle at the end of the sentence. There are two in Burmese: la: (လား), used in 'yes/no' questions, and le: (လဲ), used for all other questions.

sa:-pi:-bi-la:?	စားပြီးပြီလား။	Have you eaten yet?
na-me be-lo hkɔ-dhə-le:?	နာမည် ဘယ်လို ခေါ်သလဲ။	What's your name?

The second example also shows a case of weakening, commonly found in questions. In such cases, -te/de (တယ်) is no longer the final particle and so is substituted with the related particle, "dhə" (သ) particle which is then followed by the question particle in the final position.

Conversation 1

Bill
ဘီလ်

nei-kaun:-yẹ-la: hkə-mya:?

နေကောင်းရဲ့လား ခင်ဗျား။

How are you?.

Thi-da
သီတာ

nei-kaun:-ba-de. shin-gɔ:[4] nei-kaun:-yẹ-la:?

နေကောင်းပါတယ်။ ရှင်ကော နေကောင်းရဲ့လား

I'm fine. And how are you?

Bill
ဘီလ်

nei-kaun:-ba-de. hkə-mya: na-me be-lo hkɔ-dhə-le:?

နေကောင်းပါတယ်။ ခင်ဗျား နာမည် ဘယ်လို ခေါ်သလဲ။

I'm fine. What is your name?

Thi-da
သီတာ

jə-mạ[5] na-me thi-da-ba. twẹi-yạ-da wun:-tha-ba-de.
shin-gɔ: na-me be-lo hkɔ-dhə-le:?

ကျွန်မ နာမည် သီတာပါ။ တွေ့ရတာ ဝမ်းသာပါတယ်။
ရှင်ကော နာမည် ဘယ်လို ခေါ်သလဲ။

My name is Thida. Glad to meet you.
And what is your name?

Bill

ဘီလ်

jə-nɔ̣ na-me Bill-ba. jə-nɔ-le:
twẹi-yạ-da wun:-tha-ba-de.

ကျွန်တော့ နာမည် ဘီလ်ပါ။ ကျွန်တော်လည်း
တွေ့ရတာ ဝမ်းသာပါတယ်။

My name is Bill. I'm also glad to meet you.

---

[4] The particle -kɔ:/gɔ:, translated as "as for you", or "and you" shows emphasis.
[5] Adding a creaky tone to the end of jə-nɔ̣ converts it to the possessive form.

Conversation 2

Dan
ဒန့်

da be-lo hkɔ-dhə-le:?
ဒါ ဘယ်လို ခေါ်သလဲ။
What is this called?

Nyi-mạ-lei:[6]
ညီမလေး

e:-da na-yi hkɔ-de.
အဲဒါ နာရီ ခေါ်တယ်။
It's called a watch.

Dan
ဒန့်

di na-yi be-lau'-le:?
ဒီ နာရီ ဘယ်လောက်လဲ။
How much is this watch?

Nyi-mạ-lei:
ညီမလေး

hnə-htaun ja'-pa.
နှစ်ထောင် ကျပ်ပါ။
two thousand kyats.

Dan
ဒန့်

o, zei:-cho-de. da yu-me. di-hma pai'-hsan.
အို ဈေးချိုတယ်။ ဒါ ယူမယ်။ ဒီမှာ ပိုက်ဆံ။
Oh, that's a good price. I'll take it. Here's
the money.

Nyi-mạ-lei:
ညီမလေး

jei:-zu:-tin-ba-de.
ကျေးဇူးတင်ပါတယ်။
Thank you.

---

[6] Nyi-mạ-lei: literally means "younger sister" and is used to address waitresses,
clerks and other female workers younger than the (male) speaker. See the
grammar section of Lesson 7 for more details.

wa-ja̱-mya: ဝါကျများ   **Sentences**

1. A: da sa-o'-la:?
        ဒါ စာအုပ်လား။
        Is this a book?

    B: ho'-ke̱, da sa-o'-ba.
        ဟုတ်ကဲ့၊ ဒါ စာအုပ်ပါ။
        Yes, this is a book.

2. A: da .na-yi-la:?
        ဒါ နာရီလား။
        Is this a watch?

    B: mə-ho'-hpu:,[7] da na-yi mə-ho'-hpu:.
        မဟုတ်ဘူး၊ ဒါ နာရီ မဟုတ်ဘူး။
        No, this is not a watch.

3. A: e:-da ba-le:?
        အဲဒါ ဘာလဲ။
        What is that?

    B: e:-da ei'-ba.
        အဲဒါ အိတ်ပါ။
        That is a bag.

4. A: da hke:-dan-la:, bɔ:-pin-la:?
        ဒါ ခဲတံလား၊ ဘောပင်လား။
        Is this a pencil (or) a pen?

    B: da bɔ:-pin-ba.
        ဒါ ဘောပင်ပါ။
        This is a pen.

---

[7] The negative -hpu:/bu: (ဘူး) particle, although written using a "b" sound, is an example of an older spelling form that is pronounced as an aspirated "p" sound when not voiced.

5.   A: da be-lo hkɔ-dhə-le:?
          ဒါ ဘယ်လို ခေါ်သလဲ။
          What is that called?

     B: myei-bon-ba.
          မြေပုံပါ။
          [It's a] map, sir.

6.   A: na:-le-ye-la:?
          နားလည်ရဲ့လား။
          Do you understand?

     B: na:-le-de.
          နားလည်တယ်။
          I understand.

     C: na:-mə-le-bu:.
          နားမလည်ဘူး။
          I don't understand.

7.   A: jei:-zu:-tin-ba-de.
          ကျေးဇူးတင်ပါတယ်။
          Thank you.

     B: jei:-zu:-be:.
          ကျေးဇူးပဲ။
          Thanks.

     C: yạ-ba-de[8].
          ရပါတယ်။
          That's all right.

---

[8] yạ-ba-de, can be used to mean both "that's all right" and "no thanks." Since it can be ambiguous, it is often accompanied by a head nod or shake to indicate an affirmative or negative answer, respectively.

Numbers in Burmese

Although Arabic numerals (1, 2, 3...) are often used in Myanmar, the Burmese numbers also in common use, so you'll need to know them for signs and written materials. The numbers will be presented again in the writing section of Lesson 5.

0	thon-nyạ	၀	သုည
1	ti'	၁	တစ်
2	hni'	၂	နှစ်
3	thon:	၃	သုံး
4	lei:	၄	လေး
5	nga:	၅	ငါး
6	chau'	၆	ခြောက်
7	hkun-hni' -or- hkun[9]	၇	ခုနှစ်၊ ခွန်
8	shi'	၈	ရှစ်
9	ko:	၉	ကိုး
10	tə-hse[10]	၁၀	တစ်ဆယ်
11	hsẹ-ti'	၁၁	ဆယ်တစ်
12	hsẹ-hni'	၁၂	ဆယ့်နှစ်
16	hsẹ-chau'	၁၆	ဆယ့်ခြောက်
20	nə-hse	၂၀	နှစ်ဆယ်
21	hnə-hsẹ-ti'	၂၁	နှစ်ဆယ့်တစ်
22	hnə-hsẹ-hni'	၂၂	နှစ်ဆယ့်နှစ်
26	hnə-hsẹ-chau'	၂၆	နှစ်ဆယ့်ခြောက်

---

[9] The word hkun is used when giving a series of numbers, such as a phone number.

[10] When combined with another word, ti' (one), hni' (two) and hkun-ni' (seven) are "weakened" and instead pronounced as: tə, hnə, and hkun-hnə, respectively.

30	thon:-ze	၃၀	သုံးဆယ်
31	thon:-zẹ-ti'	၃၁	သုံးဆယ့်တစ်
32	thon:-zẹ-hni'	၃၂	သုံးဆယ့်နှစ်
40	lei:-ze	၄၀	လေးဆယ်
50	nga:-ze	၅၀	ငါးဆယ်
60	chau'-hse	၆၀	ခြောက်ဆယ်
70	hkun-hnə-hse	၇၀	ခုနှစ်ဆယ်
80	shi'-hse	၈၀	ရှစ်ဆယ်
90	ko:-ze	၉၀	ကိုးဆယ်
100	tə-ya	၁၀၀	တစ်ရာ
200	hnə-ya	၂၀၀	နှစ်ရာ
300	thon:-ya	၃၀၀	သုံးရာ
400	lei:-ya	၄၀၀	လေးရာ
500	nga:-ya	၅၀၀	ငါးရာ
600	chau'-ya	၆၀၀	ခြောက်ရာ
700	hkun-hnə-ya	၇၀၀	ခုနှစ်ရာ
800	shi'-ya	၈၀၀	ရှစ်ရာ
900	ko:-ya	၉၀၀	ကိုးရာ
1000	tə-htaun	၁၀၀၀	တစ်ထောင်
2000	hnə-htaun	၂၀၀၀	နှစ်ထောင်
10,000	tə-thaun:	၁၀၀၀၀	တစ်သောင်း
100,000	tə-thein:	၁၀၀၀၀၀	တစ်သိန်း

Test 1

Match the English words with the Burmese words.

_____	1.	watch	a.	le: လည်း
_____	2.	book	b.	bɔ:-pin ဘောပင်
_____	3.	pen	c.	na-me နာမည်
_____	4.	this	d.	hke:-dan ခဲတံ
_____	5.	I (male speaker)	e.	na-yi နာရီ
_____	6.	also	f.	da ဒါ
_____	7.	pencil	g.	jə-nɔ ကျွန်တော်
_____	8.	name	h.	di ဒီ
_____	9.	what	i.	ei' အိတ်
_____	10.	bag	j.	sa-o' စာအုပ်
			k.	ba ဘာ

Translate sentences 1-3 into English. Transliterate sentences 4-5 into Burmese.

1. ဒါ ဘာလဲ။ ဒါ နာရီပါ။

_____

2. နေကောင်းရဲ့လား။

_____

3. တွေ့ရတာ ဝမ်းသာပါတယ်။

_____

4. I'm sorry.

_____

5. This is a newspaper, right?

_____

Drills

1. Write and say the following sentences in Burmese.

How are you doing?

My name is _____.

This is a map.

This is not a pen.

2. Use the following words to help form complete sentences.

jə-mạ ကျွန်မ	e:-da အဲဒါ	ba ဘာ
jə-nɔ ကျွန်တော်	-pa/ba ပါ	ho-ha ဟိုဟာ
hkə-mya: ခင်ဗျား	ho'-kẹ ဟုတ်ကဲ့	shin ရှင်
na-yi နာရီ	da-ba-le: ဒါဘာလဲ	na-me နာမည်
bɔ:-pin ဘောပင်	mə-ho'-hpu: မဟုတ်ဘူး	-le: လဲ
thə-din:-za သတင်းစာ	nei-kaun:-ba-de နေကောင်းပါတယ်	

3. Practice saying each word in the vocabulary list in conjunction with the audio recordings. Say the word first, then wait and listen to the recording. This will tell you how accurately you are pronouncing the words. It will also help you learn the transliteration system.

Reading & Writing

The Burmese Writing System

The modern Burmese writing system, called myan-ma-za
(မြန်မာစာ), is based on the written forms of the Mon and Pyu
languages which predate the arrival Bamar peoples to what is now
Myanmar in the tenth century and were, in turn, based on writing
systems brought, along with Buddhism, from India. Modern
Burmese script includes 33 consonants, about 14 vowels, two tone
marks and a number of additional specialized characters.

Burmese is a phonetic language that is usually pronounced as it is
written, though there are many exceptions and variations that must
also be learned as well. This book covers the most important
variations of how the written language is pronounced, but it should
be kept in mind that some of the complexities of written Burmese
go well beyond the scope of this book.

The reading and writing sections in Lessons 1-5 cover the basics of
how colloquial Burmese is written. Lessons 6-9, then discuss the
most important cases of writing and pronunciation variations
including voicing, weakening and stacked consonants. The last
lesson of the book, Lesson 10, discusses the literary form of
Burmese. Literary form in Burmese varies from the spoken form in
the different particles it uses, and has many common uses, such as
in signs, dictionaries and formal correspondence, so a brief
introduction may prove helpful for a beginning student.

Although there are 33 consonants in Burmese, 8 of these are rarely
used and so will be presented in Lesson 9 along with the
uncommon vowel symbols. Also, because the last letter in the
alphabet, a (အ) is so common and begins many words, it will be
included in this first writing section which presents seven
consonants, six vowels and the two tone marks.

Practice Writing Consonants

Practice writing the following consonants. Remember to use the proper stroke order as shown below.

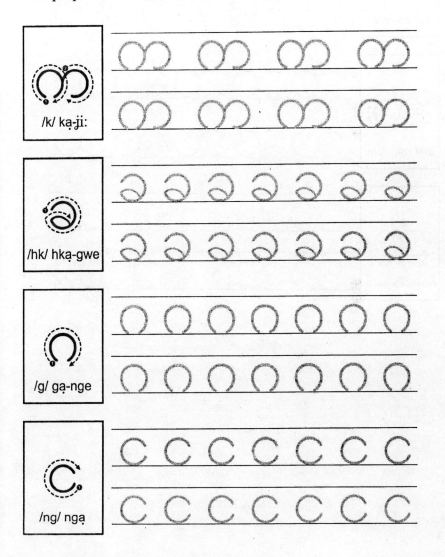

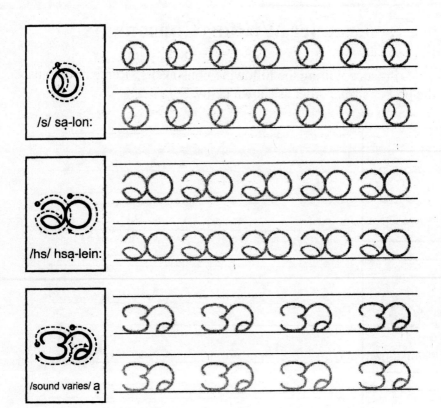

/s/ sạ-lon:

/hs/ hsạ-lein:

/sound varies/ ạ

Simple Vowels

Six simple vowels are shown below. Some vowels have two forms depending on the letter it is attached to.The long form of yei:-chạ is used in order to avoid writing something that will look like a different consonant. For example, the -pa/ba (ပါ) particle uses the long yei:-chạ to avoid looking like hạ (ဟ). Also, remember that complex vowels are written using multiple symbols that must be viewed as a unit to be pronounced correctly.

Vowel	Sound	Name
1. ⁻ ာ	/a/	yei:-chạ ‌ေရးချ
⁻ါ		yei:-chạ (long form)
2. ◌	/ị/	lon:-ji:-tin (uses creaky tone)[11] လုံးကြီးတင်
3. ◌	/i/	lon:-ji:-tin hsan-hka' လုံးကြီးတင် ဆန်ခတ်
4. ⁻	/ụ/	tə-chaun:-ngin (uses creaky tone)[11] တစ်ချောင်းငင်
⁻	/ụ/	tə-chaun:-ngin (long form)[12]
5. ⁻	/u/	hnə-chaun:-ngin နှစ်ချောင်းငင်
⁻	/u/	hnə-chaun:-ngin (long form)[12]
6. ေ ⁻	/ei/	thə-wei-hto: သ‌ေဝထိုး

---

[11] See note on page 34 regarding unmarked creaky tones.
[12] The long forms of tə-chaun:-ngin and hnə-chaun:-ngin are used if there isn't room to place the symbol in its normal position beneath a consonant.

Practice Writing the Following Vowels

Practicing writing the following vowels using အ. Remember to
always start writing a character with the small circle if there is one.

အာ   အာ   အာ   အာ

အိ   အိ   အိ   အိ

အီ   အီ   အီ   အီ

အု   အု   အု   အု

အူ   အူ   အူ   အူ

ေအာ   ေအာ   ေအာ   ေအာ

Read the Following Aloud

Note that all of these sounds below are low tones.

1.   ကာ   ကီ   ကု   ကေ

2.   ခါ   ခီ   ခု   ခေ

3.   ဂါ   ဂီ   ဂု   ဂေ

4.   ဃါ   ဃီ   ဃု   ဃေ

5.   စာ   စီ   စု   စေ

6.   ဆာ   ဆီ   ဆု   ဆေ

7.   အာ   အီ   အု   အေ

Burmese Tone Marks

Burmese has four tones which are usually, but not always, marked with special characters. The low tone is unmarked, however, and there are cases where other tones are unmarked as well. This section presents the tone marks for the high and creaky tones. The fourth, "stopped" tone is a bit more complicated, so we'll discuss it in Lesson 2.

Creaky Tone Mark (First Tone)

◦̄ /creaky tone mark/ au'-kạ-myi' အောက်ကမြစ်

Like the high tone, the creaky tone, falls from high to low, but it is shorter and falls more quickly than the high tone and also has the important characteristic of ending with a weak or gentle closure of the glottis, a bit like a gargling sound, but is quieter, very short and deeper in the throat.

Low Tone (No Mark, Second Tone)

A syllable with no tone mark is generally pronounced with a low tone. The Myanmar low tone is only relatively low compared to the other three tones, but is actually pronounced as a long, flat mid-level tone that may rise or fall slightly at the end.

High Tone Mark (Third Tone)

–ः /high tone mark/ wə-sạ-hnə-lon:-bau' ဝတ္ထုနှစ်လုံးပေါက်

The high tone is a long tone that starts high and then slowly falls to the level of the low tone. It is usually indicated by placing the above colon-like mark at the end of a syllable. Two other vowels (see Lesson 3) are also pronounced using an unmarked high tone.

Unmarked Creaky Tones

Not all tones are marked in Burmese. A syllable with no tone mark may indicate a creaky tone under some circumstances. In this lesson, you've seen two important cases of unmarked "creaky" vowels: lon:-ji:-tin ($\overset{o}{}$ pronounced as "i̱"), and tə-chaun:-ngin ($_\iota$ pronounced as "o̱"). The third common case of an unmarked creaky tone is when no vowel is indicated at all. For example, the verbs sa̱-de စတယ် (start) and ka̱-de, ကတယ် (dance) both begin with creaky tones.

Read the Following Aloud

Each row follows the same tone order: Creaky, Low, High.

1. က	ကာ	ကာ:
2. ကိ	ကီ	ကီ:
3. ကု	ကူ	ကူ:
4. ကေ့	ကေ	ကေ:
5. ə	ခါ	ခါ:
6. ဒိ	ဒီ	ဒီ:
7. ဒု	ဒူ	ဒူ:
8. ဒေ့	ဒေ	ဒေ:
9. ဂ	ဂါ	ဂါ:
10. ဝိ	ဝီ	ဝီ:

11.	၃	၃	၃း
12.	ေဂ့	ေဂ	ေဂး
13.	င	ငါ	ငါး
14.	၈	၈	၈း
15.	၃	၃	၃း
16.	ေင့	ေင	ေငး
17.	ဝ	ဝာ	ဝား
18.	၈	၈	၈း
19.	၃	၃	၃း
20.	ေစ့	ေစ	ေစး
21.	ဆ	ဆာ	ဆား
22.	ဆိ	ဆီ	ဆီး
23.	ဆု	ဆူ	ဆူး
24.	ေဆ့	ေဆ	ေဆး
25.	အ	အာ	အား
26.	အိ	အီ	အီး
27.	အု	အူ	အူး
28.	ေအ့	ေအ	ေအး

Writing Exercise 1

Write the following words and sounds in Burmese script.

1. ka: (car)   _____

2. ku: (cross (v))   _____

3. hka: (bitter or waist)   _____

4. gu (cave)   _____

5. nga: (five or fish)   _____

6. sa: (eat (v))   _____

7. si: (ride (v))   _____

8. zə-ga: (language)   _____

9. hsa: (salt)   _____

10. hsi (oil)   _____

11. hsei: (medicine or wash (v))   _____

12. a: (free, not busy (v))   _____

Lesson 2

မှာ (at); ရှိ (to have); Myanmar cities; conjunctions; present tense; negating a verb; present progressive; consonants II; and vowels; final consonant sounds

thin-gan:-za hni'   သင်ခန်းစာ ၂   Lesson 2

wɔ:-ha-rạ   ဝေါဟာရ   Vocabulary

Nouns

te-li-hpon:	တယ်လီဖုန်း	telephone
mye'-hman	မျက်မှန်	eyeglasses
pai'-hsan	ပိုက်ဆံ	money
dɔ-la	ဒေါ်လာ	dollar
ja'	ကျပ်	kyat (Myanmar currency)
pon	ပုံ	picture
da'-pon	ဓာတ်ပုံ	photograph
kin-mə-ra	ကင်မရာ	camera
ə-bị-dan	အဘိဓာန်	dictionary
se'-ku	စက္ကူ	paper
zə-bwe:	စားပွဲ	table
ei'-ya	အိပ်ရာ	bed
kə-lə-htain	ကုလားထိုင်	chair
ə-hkan:	အခန်း	room
ei'-hkan:	အိပ်ခန်း	bedroom
ein-dha	အိမ်သာ	bathroom, toilet
ein	အိမ်	house, home
lan:	လမ်း	way, road, path, street
di-hma	ဒီမှာ	here
e:-di-hma	အဲဒီမှာ	there
ho-hma	ဟိုမှာ	over there (farther away)
be	ဘယ်	which or left
be-hma	ဘယ်မှာ	where

nya	ညာ	right
be'	ဘက်	side
ə-yan:	အရမ်း	very, much
ə-mya:, ə-mya:-ji:	အများ၊ အများကြီး	many, a lot
jən-dɔ-dọ	ကျွန်တော်တို့	we (male speaker)
jə-mạ-dọ	ကျွန်မတို့	we (female speaker)
thu-dọ	သူတို့	they
pye, nain-gan	ပြည်၊ နိုင်ငံ	country
myan-ma-nain-gan	မြန်မာနိုင်ငံ	Myanmar
bə-ma-ye	ဗမာပြည်	Burma
tə-yo'-pye	တရုတ်ပြည်	China
in-gə-lan	အင်္ဂလန်	England
htain:-nain-gan	ထိုင်းနိုင်ငံ	Thailand
ein-dị-yạ	အိန္ဒိယ	India
ə-mei-rị-kạ	အမေရိက	America
ka-li-hpo:-ni:-ya:	ကာလိဖုံးနီးယား	California
jə-pan	ဂျပန်	Japan/Japanese
ba-dha-zə-ga:	ဘာသာစကား	language
myan-ma-zə-ga:	မြန်မာစကား၊	Myanmar language[13]
myan-ma-lo	မြန်မာလို	in Myanmar
bə-ma-zə-ga:	ဗမာစကား၊	Burmese language
bə- ma-zə-lo	ဗမာလို	in Burmese
tə-yo'-sə-ga:	တရုတ်စကား	Chinese language
in:-gə-lei'-sə-ga:	အင်္ဂလိပ်စကား	English language

---

[13] bə-ma-zə-ga: and myan-ma-ze-ga: are used more or less interchangeably in common speech. The -sa/za စာ particle is used for the written form of a language (see Lesson 3).

pyin-thi'-sə-ga:	ပြင်သစ်စကား	French language
ja-man-zə-ga:	ဂျာမန်စကား	German language
-lu	လူ	person
-lu-dwei	လူတွေ	people
-myo:	မျိုး	kind, type, category
-lu-myo:	လူမျိုး	nationality, ethnicity

Verbs

yai'-te	ရိုက်တယ်	to take [a photo]
la-de	လာတယ်	to come
la-gẹ	လာခဲ့	Come here!
nei-de	နေတယ်	to live or stay somewhere
shị-de	ရှိတယ်	to have
thin-de	သင်တယ်	to study, learn
pyɔ:-de	ပြောတယ်	to speak
hke'-te	ခက်တယ်	to be difficult
lwe-de	လွယ်တယ်	to be easy

Particles

-hma	မှာ	in, at
-nẹ	နဲ့	and, with
-kạ/gạ	က	from
-sheị	ရှေ့	front
nau'-	နောက်	back
ə-pɔ	အပေါ်	on
-au'	အောက်	under
-ja:	ကြား	between
-zə-ga:	စကား	language (suffix)
-lo	လို	in a lang., "in Burmese"

-yẹ	ရဲ့	possessive particle
mə-...-hpu:/bu:	မ[verb]ဘူး	negative particles (used in negating a sentence)

Myanmar Cities

Myanmar made up of fourteen parts; seven divisions (tain:, တိုင်း) and seven states (ne, နယ်). The divisions are regions where the main population is ethnic Burmese; such as Mandalay Division. The states are named after a local ethnic group that usually forms the main population in that area, such as northern Kachin State. Below is a list of Myanmar's larger cities.

bə-gan	ပုဂံ	Bagan
bə-go:	ပဲခူး	Bago/Pegu
bə-mɔ	ဗန်းမော်	Bhamo
jain:-ton	ကျိုင်းတုံ	Kyaingtong//Kengtung
la:-sho:	လားရှိုး	Lashio
man:-də-lei:	မန္တလေး	Mandalay
mɔ-lə-myain	မော်လမြိုင်	Moulmein
bei'	မြိတ်	Myeik/Mergui
myi'-ji:-na:	မြစ်ကြီးနား	Myitkyina
nyaun-u:	ညောင်ဦး	Nyaung-U
nyaun-shwei	ညောင်ရွှေ	Nyaungshwe
hpa:-an	ဘားအံ	Pa-an
sə-gain:	စစ်ကိုင်း	Sagaing
si'-twẹi	စစ်တွေ	Sittwe
taun-ji:	တောင်ကြီး	Taunggyi
də-we	ထားဝယ်	Tavoy/Dawei
yan-gon	ရန်ကုန်	Yangon/Rangoon

thə-da   သဒ္ဒါ   **Grammar**

Burmese has three main categories of words: nouns, verbs and particles. Particles exist only as "bound" forms and must be added as prefixes, suffixes or infixes to the words they modify. Particles play many roles, such as to indicate politeness (Lesson 1), conjunctions (see below) and verb forms (Lesson 3).

Noun Particles: -nẹ နဲ့ **(and), -le:** လည်း **(also), -hma** မှာ **(at)**

So far, I've introduced a few of the more common conjunctions. Most Burmese conjunctions are particles, attached to a noun as suffixes. For example:

If the word for *which*:	be	ဘယ်
along with the particle for *at*:	-hma	မှာ
forms "which + at" or *where*:	be-hma	ဘယ်မှာ

Other conjunctions introduced so far include:

-nẹ	နဲ့	and, with, between
-le:	လည်း	also, and (when used with two verbs)
-hma	မှာ	at, in, from[14]

Verb Particle: -te/de တယ် (Present/Past)

The most common verb form is the present/past. It is formed by adding the particle -te တယ်, usually voiced as "-de" to the verb root. For example,

the verb for understand is: na:-le   နားလည်

---

[14] location words also use -hma. E.g.,, here: di ဒီ + -hma မှာ (at) = di-hma ဒီမှာ

Then: [I/you/he/she] understand(s) is: na:-le-de   နားလည်တယ်

Some other common verbs are:

  [I/you/he/she] go(es)   thwa:-de   သွားတယ်
  [I/you/he/she] come(s)   la-de   လာတယ်
  [I/you/he/she] eat(s)   sa:-de   စားတယ်

-te is usually voiced (pronounced as -de), *except* when it follows a
glottal stop, as in:

  [I/you/he/she] like(s)   jai'-te   ကြိုက်တယ်

Note that when the present/past particle is not in the final position
in the verb phrase, it changes form to thə/dhə (သ) :

  [Do you] like [it]?   jai'-te-la:?   ကြိုက်သလား

Descriptive Verbs

Burmese uses "descriptive verbs" in place of adjectives. For
example, the adjective "easy" needs to be thought of as the verb
"to be easy". Such verbs use verb particles just like any other verb.
So, to say something is good, easy or difficult, you say:

  [It] is good.   kaun:-de   ကောင်းတယ်။
  [It] is easy.   lwe-de.   လွယ်တယ်။
  [It] is difficult. hke'-te.   ခက်တယ်။

Verb Particles: mə-...-hpu:/bu: မ...ဘူး (Negating a verb)

A sentence can be negated by adding the particles mạ (မ) and -hpu:/bu: (ဘူး) before and after the verb, rather like "ne...pas" in French. For example:

[I] have [something].   shị-de   ရှိတယ်

becomes:

[I] don't have [something]. mə-shị-bu: မရှိဘူး။

In some cases, the mạ particle is prefixed to the second syllable of a verb. For example, na-le:, which is actually a compound verb, is negated as:

[I] don't understand.   na:-**mə-le-bu:**   နားမလည်ဘူး။

Similarly, the phrase for saying, "I am not well" is:

[I] am not well.   nei-**mə**-kaun:-**bu:**   နေမကောင်းဘူး။

Irregularly formed negatives are discussed in more detail in Lesson 10.

Using the Verb nei နေ to form the present progressive

The present progressive (describing an action that is "in progress", such as: "he is going", "I am eating", etc.) is formed by adding "nei" (နေ) between the verb and present/past suffix. For example,

in:-gə-lei'-sə-ga: **thin-de**. အင်္ဂလိပ်စကား သင်တယ်။
[I] study English.

rewritten in the present progressive would be:

in:-gə-lei'-sə-ga: **thin-nei-de** အင်္ဂလိပ်စကား သင်နေတယ်။
[I am] studying English.

Conversation 1

Mạ Nyuṇ ba-lu-myo:-le:?
မညွန့် ဘာလူမျိုးလဲ။
What country are you from?[15]

Tom ə-mei-ri̥-kan-lu-myo:-ba. hkə-mya:-gɔ: ba-lu-myo:-le:?
တောမ် အမေရိကန်လူမျိုးပါ။ ခင်ဗျားကော ဘာလူမျိုးလဲ။
I am American. Where are you from?

Mạ Nyuṇ jə-mạ myan-ma-lu-myo:-ba. yan-gon-hma nei-ba-de.
shin-gɔ: be-hma nei-dhə-le:?
မညွန့် ကျွန်မ မြန်မာလူမျိုးပါ။ ရန်ကုန်မှာ နေပါတယ်။
ရှင်ကော ဘယ်မှာ နေသလဲ။
I am a Myanmar. [I] live in Yangon.
And where do you live?

Tom jə-nɔ ka-li-hpo:-ni:-ya:-hma nei-de.
တောမ် ကျွန်တော် ကာလီဖိုးနီးယားမှာ နေတယ်။
I live in California.

---

[15] ba lu-myo:-le: literally means "What nationality are you?"

Conversation 2

Sein   ba thin-nei-dhə-le:?
စိန်   ဘာ သင်နေသလဲ။
         What are [you] studying?

Lisa   bə-ma-zə-ga: thin-nei-de.
လီစာ   ဗမာစကား သင်နေတယ်။
         [I am] studying Burmese.

Sein   bə-ma-zə-ga hke'-thə-la:?
စိန်   ဗမာစကား ခက်သလား။
         Is Burmese difficult [to learn]?

Lisa   mə-hke'-hpu:. bə-ma-zə-ga: lwe-de.
         shin-gɔ: ba thin-nei-dhə-le:?
လီစာ   မခက်ဘူး။ ဗမာစကား လွယ်တယ်။
         ရှင်ကော ဘာ သင်နေသလဲ။
         No. Myanmar is easy. What are you studying?

Sein   tə-yo'-sə-ga: thin-nei-de. mə-lwe-bu:.
စိန်   တရုတ်စကား သင်နေတယ်။ မလွယ်ဘူး။
         [I am] studying Chinese. [It's] not easy [to
         learn].

wa-ja-mya: ဝါကျများ   Sentences

1. A: bɔ:-pin be-hma-le:
         ဘောပင် ဘယ်မှာလဲ။
         Where is the pen?

    B: di-hma.
         ဒီမှာ။
         [The pen is] here.

2. A: ə-bi-dan be-hma-le:?
         အဘိဓာန် ဘယ်မှာလဲ။
         Where is the dictionary?

    B: ə-bi-dan kə-lə-htain-bɔ-hma shi-de.
         အဘိဓာန် ကုလားထိုင်ပေါ်မှာ ရှိတယ်။
         The dictionary is on the chair.

    C: da'-pon yai'-mə-la:?
         ဓာတ်ပုံ ရိုက်မလား။
         [Can I] take a photograph?

    D: yai'-me.
         ရိုက်မယ်။
         [Yes,] take [it].

3. A: ko-htun: be-hma-le:?
         ကိုထွန်း ဘယ်မှာလဲ။
         Where is Ko Tun?

B: ko-tun: in-gə-lan-hma shị-de.
ကိုထွန်း အင်္ဂလန်မှာ ရှိတယ်။
Ko Tun is in England.

4. A: mye'-hman be-hma-le:?
မျက်မှန် ဘယ်မှာလဲ။
Where are the eyeglasses?

B: mye'-hman ei'-ya-bɔ-hma.
မျက်မှန် အိပ်ရာပေါ်မှာ။
The eyeglasses are on the bed.

5. A: kə-lə-htain be-hma-le:?
ကုလားထိုင် ဘယ်မှာလဲ။
Where is the chair?

B: kə-lə-htain ei'-hkan:-hma shị-de.
ကုလားထိုင် အိပ်ခန်းမှာ ရှိတယ်။
The chair is in the bedroom.

6. A: myan-ma-nain-ngan be-hma-le:?
မြန်မာနိုင်ငံ ဘယ်မှာလဲ။
Where is Myanmar?

B: myan-ma-nain-ngan htain:-nẹ ein-dị-ya-ja:-hma shị-de.
မြန်မာနိုင်ငံ ထိုင်းနဲ့ အိန္ဒိယကြားမှာ ရှိတယ်။
Myanmar is between Thailand and India.

7. A: ein-dha be-hma-le:?
အိမ်သာ ဘယ်မှာလဲ။
Where is the bathroom?

B: ein-dha ə-nau'-hma-la:?
အိမ်သာ အနောက်မှာလား။
Is the bathroom in the back?

C: ho'-kẹ, ein-dha ə-nau'-hma shị-de.
ဟုတ်ကဲ့၊ အိမ်သာ အနောက်မှာ ရှိတယ်။
Yes, the bathroom is in the back.

D: mə-ho'-hpu:. ein-dha nya-be'-hma.
မဟုတ်ဘူး။ အိမ်သာ ညာဘက်မှာ။
No. The bathroom is on the right side.

9. A: thụ-hma ba shị-le:?
သူ့မှာ ဘာ ရှိလဲ။
What does she have?

B: thụ-hma kin-mə-ra shị-de.
သူ့မှာ ကင်မရာ ရှိတယ်။
She has a camera.

10. A: thụ ein-hma ein-dha shị-dhə-la:?
သူ့ အိမ်မှာ အိမ်သာ ရှိသလား။
Does his house have a bathroom?

B: ho'-kẹ, thụ ein-hma ein-dha shị-de.
ဟုတ်ကဲ့၊ သူ့ အိမ်မှာ အိမ်သာ ရှိတယ်။
Yes, his house has a bathroom.

11. A: mə-sein-yẹ ei'-hkan:-hma ba shị-le?
မစိန်ရဲ့ အိပ်ခန်းမှာ ဘာ ရှိလဲ။
What does Sein have in her bedroom?

B: ma̤-sein-ye̤ ei-hkan:-hma zə-bwe:-ne̤, kə-lə-htain-ne̤ ei'-ya shi̤-de.
မစိန်ရဲ့ အိပ်ခန်းမှာ စားပွဲနဲ့ ကုလားထိုင်နဲ့ အိပ်ရာ ရှိတယ်။
Sein's bedroom has a table and a chair and a bed.

12. A: thu in:-gə-lei'-sə-ga: thin-nei-la:?
သူ အင်္ဂလိပ်စကား သင်နေလား။
Is she studying English?

B: ho'-ke̤, in:-gə-lei'-sə-ga: thin-nei-de.
ဟုတ်ကဲ့၊ အင်္ဂလိပ်စကား သင်နေတယ်။
Yes, she is learning English.

C: mə-ho'-hpu:. in:-gə-lei'-sə-ga: mə-thin-bu:.
မဟုတ်ဘူး။ အင်္ဂလိပ်စကား မသင်ဘူး။
No. She is not learning English.

13. A: bə-ma-zə-ga: be-hma thin-le:?
ဗမာစကား ဘယ်မှာ သင်လဲ။
Where did she learn Burmese?

B: thu ein-hma ə-bi̤-dan-ga̤ bə-ma-zə-ga: thin-de.
သူ အိမ်မှာ အဘိဓာန်က ဗမာစကား သင်တယ်။
She learned Burmese at home from a dictionary.

14. A: ma̤-nan-da ba thin-nei-le:?
မနန္ဒာ ဘာ သင်နေလဲ။
What is Nanda studying?

B: ma̤-nan-da pyin-thi'-sə-ga: thin-nei-de.
မနန္ဒာ ပြင်သစ်စကား သင်နေတယ်။
Nanda is studying French.

Drills

1. Write and say the following sentences in Burmese.

The map is under the table.

I speak French.

Are you studying Burmese?

Sein is in Yangon.

2. Using the transliteration system in this book, write a paragraph in Burmese answering the following questions:

- Where are you from?
- Where do you live?
- What language are you studying?
- Is the language easy or difficult?

3. Use the following words to help form ten sentences.

jə-mạ ကျွန်မ	ein-dha အိမ်သာ	ein အိမ်
jə-nɔ ကျွန်တော်	nei-de နေတယ်	-kạ/gạ က
ba �‌ဘာ	be-hma ဘယ်မှာ	be ဘယ်
hkə-mya: ခင်ဗျား	-pɔ-hma ပေါ်မှာ	nya ညာ
hsɔ:-ri:-nɔ ဆောရီးနော်	ja: ကြား	hke' ခက်
te-li-hpon: တယ်လီဖုန်း	lan: လမ်း	lwe လွယ်
ei'-ya အိပ်ရာ	thin-de သင်တယ်	yai'-te ရိုက်တယ်
ei'-hkan: အိပ်ခန်း	shị-de ရှိတယ်	-hma မှာ
kə-lə-htain ကုလားထိုင်	thu သူ	
in:-gə-lei'-sə-ga: အင်္ဂလိပ်စကား		

Test 2

Match the English words with the Burmese words.

_____	1.	left	a. be ဘယ်
_____	2.	room	b. ho-hma ဟိုမှာ
_____	3.	paper	c. lu-dwe လူတွေ
_____	4.	house	d. thin-de သင်တယ်
_____	5.	eyeglasses	e. lan: လမ်း
_____	6.	easy	f. la-de လာတယ်
_____	7.	bed	g. ei'-ya အိပ်ရာ
_____	8.	difficult	h. ja: ကျား
_____	9.	study	i. mye'-hman မျက်မှန်
_____	10.	between	j. hke' ခက်
_____	11.	come	k. zə-bwe: စားပွဲ
_____	12.	money	l. nya ညာ
_____	13.	street	m. lwe-de လွယ်တယ်
_____	14.	table	n. ein အိမ်
_____	15.	dictionary	o. se'-ku စက္ကူ
			p. ə-hkan: အခန်း
			q. ə-bị-dan အဘိဓာန်
			r. pai'-hsan ပိုက်ဆံ

Translate sentences 1-3 into English and transliterate sentences 4-5 into Burmese.

1. သူ ဗမာစကား သင်နေတယ်။

_____

2. သူ ဟိုမှာ သင်နေတယ်။

_____

3. ကျွန်မ ဂျပန်မှာ နေတယ်။

_____

4. Where is the bathroom?

_____

5. The eyeglasses are on the table.

_____

Practice Writing Consonants

Practice writing the following consonants. Remember to use the proper stroke order as shown below.

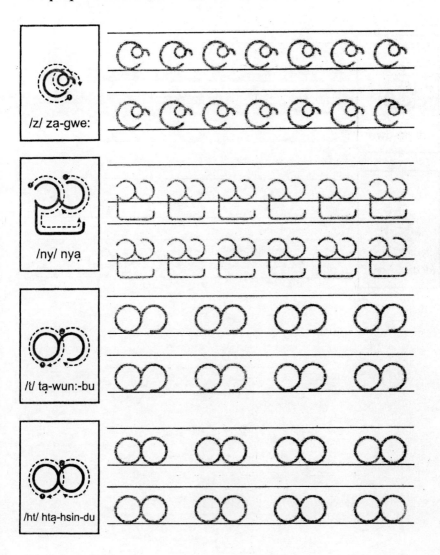

Practice Writing Consonants

Practice writing the following consonants. Remember to use the proper stroke order as shown below.

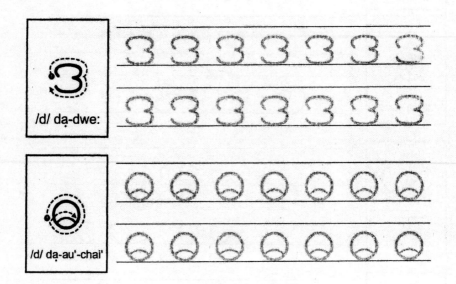

/d/ dạ-dwe:

/d/ dạ-au'-chai'

Read the Following Aloud

1. စာ စိ စီ စု စူ စေ

2. စ့ စာ စား

3. ညာ ညိ ညီ ညု ညူ

4. ည့ ညာ ညား

5. တာ တိ တီ တု တူ တေ

6. တ့ တာ တား

7. ထာ ထိ ထီ ထု ထူ ထေ

8. ထ့ ထာ ထား

9. ဒါ ဒိ ဒီ ဒု ဒူ ဒေ

10. ဒ့ါ ဒါ ဒါး

11. ဓာ ဓိ ဓီ ဓု ဓူ ဓေ

12. ဓ့ ဓာ ဓား

Final Consonants

်   ə-tha'   /final consonant mark

Burmese has just two final consonants, the nasal n and the glottal stop. Both are marked by using the ə-tha' or "killer stoke" which looks like a superscript "c". The glottal stop is the fourth tone in Burmese, but the nasal n can be combined with any of the other three tones. Both final consonants have four instances as shown below[16].

Note that the vowels sounds shown below only apply to simple vowels such as အက် (e') and not to complex vowels such as အိုက် (ai').

Final Nasal N

Consonant	Name	Pronunciation
င့် ၊ င် ၊ င်း	ngạ-tha'	iṇ/in/in:
ည့် ၊ ည် ၊ ည်း	nyạ-tha'	ẹ/e/e: (has no final n sound)
န့် ၊ န် ၊ န်း	nạ-tha'	aṇ/an/an:
မ့် ၊ မ် ၊ မ်း	mạ-tha'	aṇ/an/an: (same sound as န်)

[16] The ə-tha' symbol is also used with other letters, esp. in words of Pali or Sanskrit origin. In such cases, they don't result in a closed syllable, such as with yạ-tha' ယ်, used in the present/past verb ending as in "he goes" သူ သွားတယ်, or as in the Pali-derived word for captain or officer, bo-ji: ဗိုလ်ကြီး, that includes a silent lạ-tha' လ်.

The final nasal n is written by placing an ə-tha' above the characters င, ဋ or ဏ. The nasal n in Burmese is pronounced rather like the the first n in "un-hunh", but very short, ending almost at the beginning of the sound, so no resonance can be heard. Ngạ-tha', nạ-tha' and mạ-tha' are all pronounced in this way. Nyạ-tha' ဥ်, although listed as a final n, is pronounced as an 'e' sound, without voicing the final nasal n.

Final Stopped Tone

Consonant	Name	Pronunciation
က်	kạ-tha'	e'
စ်	sạ-tha'	i'
တ်	tạ-tha'	a'
ပ်	pạ-tha'	a' (same sound as တ်)

An ə-tha' is placed above the characters က, စ, တ or ပ, to indicate a glottal stop. This is both a vowel and the fourth, or stopped, tone. The stopped tone is also the shortest tone. It starts high, falls briefly and ends with a glottal stop.

Practice Writing the Following Vowel

Tone and Final Consonants Groups

nga-tha' (iṇ-in-in:)

အင့်   အင့်   အင့်   အင့်

အင်   အင်   အင်   အင်

အင်း   အင်း   အင်း   အင်း

nya-tha' (ẹ-e-e:)

အည့်   အည့်   အည့်   အည့်

အည်   အည်   အည်   အည်

အည်း   အည်း   အည်း   အည်း

nạ-tha' (ạn-an-an:)

အနဲ့   အနဲ့   အနဲ့   အနဲ့

အနဲ   အနဲ   အနဲ   အနဲ

အနဲး   အနဲး   အနဲး   အနဲး

mạ-tha' (ạn-an-an:)

အမဲ့   အမဲ့   အမဲ့   အမဲ့

အမဲ   အမဲ   အမဲ   အမဲ

အမဲး   အမဲး   အမဲး   အမဲး

ka̤-tha'/sa̤-tha'/ta̤-tha'/pa̤-tha' (e'/i'/a'/a')

အက်   အက်   အက်   အက်

အစ်   အစ်   အစ်   အစ်

အတ်   အတ်   အတ်   အတ်

အပ်   အပ်   အပ်   အပ်

Writing Exercise 2

Write the following words and sounds in Burmese script.

1. ko: (nine) _____

2. kaun: (good) _____

3. hkaun: (head, pron. gaun:) _____

4. gi-ṭa̱ (music) _____

5. sa-dai' (post office) _____

6. saun: (harp) _____

7. sə-ka' (skirt) _____

8. hsain (store/shop) _____

9. hso: (bad) _____

10. ze' (ferry) _____

11. zi' (zipper) _____

12. nya (right) _____

13. nyi (younger brother) _____

14. ti' (one) _____

15. tu (chopsticks) _____

16. htu (thick) _____

17. htain (sit) _____

18. htain: (Thai) _____

19. da: (knife) _____

20. ə-tu-du (same) _____

Lesson 3

going places; common verbs; lo-jin လိုချင် (to want),
thwa: သွား (to go); ; verb modes (future, past
perfect); descriptive verbs; phrases for yes and no;
complex vowels; unmarked high tones;
common consonants III

thin-gan:-za thon: သင်ခန်းစာ ၃ Lesson 3
wɔ:-ha-ṛa ဝေါဟာရ Vocabulary

Nouns

zei:	ဈေး	market
ho-te	ဟိုတယ်	hotel
hpə-ya:	ဘုရား	pagoda, (buddhist) temple[17]
jaun:	ကျောင်း	school
hpon:-ji:-jaun:	ဘုန်းကြီးကျောင်း	monastery
te'-kə-tho	တက္ကသိုလ်	university
sa-thin-gan:	စာသင်ခန်း	classroom
pan:-jan	ပန်းခြံ	park
dai'	တိုက်	brick building
sa-ji-dai'	စာကြည့်တိုက်	library
sa-dai'	စာတိုက်	post office
ban-dai'	ဘဏ်တိုက်	bank
ə-sa:, ə-sa:-ə-sa	အစား ၊ အစားအစာ	food
htə-min:	ထမင်း	cooked rice
hsain	ဆိုင်	store
htə-min:-zain	ထမင်းဆိုင်	restaurant
sa:-thau'-hsain	စားသောက်ဆိုင်	restaurant
la'-hpe'-ye-zain	လက်ဖက်ရည်ဆိုင်	tea shop
hkau'-swe:-zain	ခေါက်ဆွဲဆိုင်	noodle shop
mon-zain	မုန့်ဆိုင်	bakery
sa-o'-hsain	စာအုပ်ဆိုင်	bookstore

[17] This Pali-derived word is pronounced with an aspirated 'p' sound (hp) instead of a 'b' sound.

hsei:-yon	ဆေးရုံ	hospital
yo'-shin	ရုပ်ရှင်	movie
yo'-shin-yon	ရုပ်ရှင်ရုံ	movie theater, cinema
yon:	ရုံး	office
than-yon:	သံရုံး	embassy
di-lo-hso	ဒီလိုဆို	"in that case"
e:-di-lo-hso	အဲဒီလိုဆို	"in that case"
ti-bi, ti-bwi	တီဗီ၊ တီဗွီ	television
a:-gə-za:	အားကစား	sports, athletics
gi-tạ	ဂီတ	music
thə-chin:	သီချင်း	song(s)
e'-hkə-ya	အက္ခရာ	alphabet, script
myan-ma e'-hkə-ya	မြန်မာ အက္ခရာ	Myanmar alphabet
sa	စာ	written language, writing, letters, lessons
myan-ma-za	မြန်မာစာ	written Myanmar
in:-gə-lei' e'-hkə-ya	အင်္ဂလိပ် အက္ခရာ	English alphabet
htain: e'-hkə-ya	ထိုင်း အက္ခရာ	Thai alphabet
htain:-za	ထိုင်းစာ	written Thai
tə-chọ	တချို့	some
ne:-ne:	နည်းနည်း	a little bit, small amount

Verbs

thwa:-de	သွားတယ်	to go
pyan-de	ပြန်တယ်	to go back, return
na:-htaun-de	နားထောင်တယ်	to listen
lo-ɟin-de	လိုချင်တယ်	to want

we-de	ဝယ်တယ်	to buy
sa:-de	စားတယ်	to eat
lo'-te	လုပ်တယ်	to do, make
ə-lo'-lo'-te	အလုပ်လုပ်တယ်	to work
jai'-te	ကြိုက်တယ်	to like, prefer
ji -de	ကြည့်တယ်	to watch, look at
htain-de	ထိုင်တယ်	to sit
ei'-te	အိပ်တယ်	to sleep, lie down
lai'-te	လိုက်တယ်	to follow, go with
nain-de, ta'-te	နိုင်တယ် ၊ တတ်တယ်	can, be able to, know how to do
le'-hkan-de	လက်ခံတယ်	to receive
gə-za:-de	ကစားတယ်	to play
hpa'-te	ဖတ်တယ်	to read
yei:-de	ရေးတယ်	to write
kaun:-de	ကောင်းတယ်	to be good
hso:-de	ဆိုးတယ်	to be bad, naughty
thei'	သိပ်	very (adverb)

tha-da   သဒ္ဒါ   Grammar

Verb Particle: -me မယ် (Future)

Future action is indicated by adding -me (မယ်) to a verb. Thus, "I will go" is written:

[I] will go/[I'm going to go]   thwa:-me   သွားမယ်॥

When the "-me" particle is not at the end of the verb phrase, it changes to "mə" (မ):

Will [you] follow?   lai'-mə-la:? လိုက်မလား॥

Verb Particle: -bi ပြီ (Past Perfect)

The past perfect is the verb form that describes a completed action. In Burmese, this is formed by adding -pi/-bi to the verb. For example:

[I] have eaten.   sa:-bi   စား ပြီ॥

Frequently the verb pi: (ပြီး), meaning "finished", is added to the end of a verb, which is used in the same way that the adverbs "yet" and "already" are used in English:

Have [you] eaten yet (already)? sa:-pi:-bi-la:? စားပြီးပြီလား॥
Yes, [I've] already eaten.
                ho'-kẹ, sa:-pi:-bi   ဟုတ်ကဲ့၊ စားပြီးပြီ॥

This form is also used to indicate a complete action:

[I] went to the store (& came back). ·
                hsain-ko thwa:-pi:-bi   ဆိုင်ကိုသွားပြီးပြီ॥

Yes and No

A number of expressions are used to convey meanings similar to "yes" and "no". The examples listed below can all be heard in common speech.

ho'-kẹ	ဟုတ်ကဲ့	Yes (lit., "that's correct").
ho'-te	ဟုတ်တယ်	Yes (informal).
in:	အင်း	Yes (very informal).
yạ-ba-de	ရပါတယ်	That's all right.[18]
kaun:-bi	ကောင်းပြီ	That's fine.
də-ge-ba	တကယ်ပါ	Certainly, really.
hman-de	မှန်တယ်	That's correct.
thə-bɔ-tu-de	သဘောတူတယ်	[I] agree.
mə-ho'-hpu:.	မဟုတ်ဘူး	No/Not so.
hiṇ in:	ဟင့်အင်း	No (very informal).
mə-yạ-bu:	မရဘူး	That's not all right.
hma:-de	မှားတယ်	That's wrong.
thə-bɔ-mə-tu-bu:	သဘောမတူဘူး	[I] disagree.

---

[18] Can be used to mean either, "yes, that's all right" or "no, thanks.". Make sure to nod or shake your head to make your intention clear if you use this phrase.

Conversation 1

Zaw be-thwa:-ɟin-dhə-le:?
ဇော် ဘယ်သွားချင်သလဲ။
Where do [you] want to go?

John yo'-shin thwa:-ɟi̱-ɟin-de.
ဂျွန် ရုပ်ရှင် သွားကြည့်ချင်တယ်။
[I] want to go and watch a movie.

Zaw jə-nɔ yo'-shin mə-ɟi̱-ɟin-bu:.
ဇော် ကျွန်တော် ရုပ်ရှင် မကြည့်ချင်ဘူး။
[I] don't want to watch a movie.

John di-lo-hso, be-thwa:-ɟin-dhə-le:?
ဂျွန် ဒီလိုဆို ဘယ်သွားချင်သလဲ။
In that case, where would [you] like to go?

Zaw: la'-hpe'-ye-zain thwa:-ɟin-de. lai'-mə-la:?
ဇော် လက်ဖက်ရည်ဆိုင် သွားချင်တယ်။ လိုက်မလား။
[I] want to go to a teashop. Like to come along?[19]

John kaun:-bi. lai'-me.
ဂျွန် ကောင်းပြီ။ လိုက်မယ်။
That's fine. [I] will follow [you].

---

[19] Literally, "Will [you] follow?"

Conversation 2

Thet   bə-ma-zə-ga: pyɔ:-da'-thə-la:?
သက်   ဗမာစကား ပြောတတ်သလား။
         Can [you] speak Burmese?

Jill   ho'-kẹ, bə-ma-zə-ga: ne:-ne: pyɔ:-da'-te.
ဂျီလ်း   ဟုတ်ကဲ့၊ ဗမာစကား နည်းနည်း ပြောတတ်တယ်။
         Yes, [I] can speak a little Burmese.

Thet   thei' kaun:-de.
သက်   သိပ် ကောင်းတယ်။
         [That's] very good.

Thet   bə-ma-zə-ga: be-hma thin-dhə-le:?
သက်   ဗမာစကား ဘယ်မှာ သင်သလဲ။
         Where did [you] study Burmese?

Jill   myan-ma-lu-myo:-nẹ htain:-hma thin-de.
ဂျီလ်း   မြန်မာလူမျိုးနဲ့ ထိုင်းမှာ သင်တယ်။
         I studied with Myanmar people in Thailand.

Thet   myan-ma-za-le: yei:-da'-thə-la:?
သက်   မြန်မာစာလည်း ရေးတတ်သလား။
         Can [you] also write in Myanmar?

Jill   ho'-kẹ, myan-ma-za ne:-ne: yei:-da'-te.
ဂျီလ်း   ဟုတ်ကဲ့ မြန်မာစာ နည်းနည်း ရေးတတ်တယ်။
         Yes, [I] can write in Myanmar a little bit.

wa-ja-mya: ဝါကျများ   Sentences

1.   A: be-thwa:-mə-le:?
          ဘယ်သွားမလဲ။
          Where are you going?

     B: zei: thwa:-me.
          ဈေး သွားမယ်။
          I am going to the market.

     C: sa-o'-hsain thwa:-me.
          စာအုပ်ဆိုင် သွားမယ်။
          I am going to the bookstore.

2.   A: ba we-jin-dhə-le:?
          ဘာ ဝယ်ချင်သလဲ။
          What would you like to buy?

     B: bə-gan myei-bon we-jin-de.
          ပုဂံ မြေပုံ ဝယ်ချင်တယ်။
          I want to buy a map of Bagan.

3.   A: thu ba lo'-chin-dhə-le:?
          သူ ဘာ လုပ်ချင်သလဲ။
          What does she want to do?

     B: thu thə-chin: na:-htaun-jin-de.
          သူ သီချင်း နားထောင်ချင်တယ်။
          She wants to listen to music.

4.   A: pan:-jan thwa:-jin-dhə-la:?
ပန်းခြံ သွားချင်သလား။
Do you want to go to the park?

B: mə-thwa:-jin-bu:. sa-dai' thwa:-jin-de.
မသွားချင်ဘူး။ စာတိုက် သွားချင်တယ်။
No. I want to go to the post office.

5.   A: be-hma sa:-jin-dhə-le:?
ဘယ်မှာ စားချင်သလဲ။
Where would you like to eat?

B: hkau'-hswe:-zain-hma thwa:-sa:-jin-de.
ခေါက်ဆွဲဆိုင်မှာ သွားစားချင်တယ်။
I want to go eat at a noodle shop.

C: ein-hma pyan-sa:-jin-de.
အိမ်မှာ ပြန်စားချင်တယ်။
I want to go back and eat at home.

6.   A: ein-dha thwa:-jin-de
အိမ်သာ သွားချင်တယ်။
[I] want to go to the bathroom.

B: yạ-ba-de. ə-nau'-hma shị-de.
ရပါတယ်။ အနောက်မှာ ရှိတယ်။
That's okay. It's in the back.

C: mə-yạ-bu:.
မရဘူး။
That's not all right.

7. A: hpə-ya: thwa:-jin-de.
ဘုရား သွားချင်တယ်။
I want to go to the temple.

B: ya̰-ba-de.
ရပါတယ်။
That's all right.

8. A: ba ba-dha-zə-ga: pyɔ:-da'-thə-le:?
ဘာ ဘာသာစကား ပြောတတ်သလဲ။
What languages can you speak?

B: in:-gə-lei'-nḛ bə-ma-zə-ga: pyɔ:-da'-te.
အင်္ဂလိပ်နဲ့ ဗမာစကား ပြောတတ်တယ်။
I can speak English and Burmese.

9. A: htain:-za yei:-da'-thə-la:?
ထိုင်းစာ ရေးတတ်သလား။
Can you write in Thai?

B: htain:-za ne:-ne: yei:-da'-te.
ထိုင်းစာ နည်းနည်း ရေးတတ်တယ်။
I can write a little Thai.

C: mə-yei:-da'-hpu:. htain:-za mə-yei:-da'-hpu:.
မရေးတတ်ဘူး။ ထိုင်းစာ မရေးတတ်ဘူး။
No, I can't. I can't write in Thai.

Drills

1. Write and say the following sentences in (transliterated) Burmese.

I'm going to a teashop. Will come you along?

Come to my house. It'sin front of the school.

Have you eaten already? Yes, I ate a lot.

Ma Thet comes from Bago Division.

2. Choose four buildings or shops and write a (transliterated) Burmese sentence about each one describing where it's located, or what you will do there.

3. Use the following words to help form ten sentences.

jaun: ကျောင်း   we-de ဝယ်တယ်   yo'-shin-yon ရုပ်ရှင်ရုံ

thei' သိပ်   sa:-de စားတယ်   ei'-te အိပ်တယ်

be-hma ဘယ်မှာ   tə-chọ တချို့   htə-min:-zain

be ဘယ်   ə-sa: အစား   ne:-ne: နည်းနည်း

lo'-te လုပ်တယ်   hpa'-te ဖတ်တယ်   sa-dai' စာတိုက်

lan: လမ်း   yei:-de ရေးတယ်   sa-o'-hsain စာအုပ်ဆိုင်

thwa:-de သွားတယ်   shị-de ရှိတယ်   sa-thin-gan: စာသင်ခန်း

pyɔ:-de ပြောတယ်   jai'-te ကြိုက်တယ်   lo-jin-de လိုချင်တယ်

-hma မှာ   hsei:-yon ဆေးရုံ   myan-ma-e'-hkə-ya
                                              နံမာအက္ခရာ

Test 3

Match the English words with the Burmese words.

_____ 1.   sleep   a. lo-jin-de လိုချင်တယ်

_____ 2.   some   b. yo'-shin-yon ရုပ်ရှင်ရုံ

_____ 3.   hospital   c. gi-ta̩ ဂီတ

_____ 4.   market   d. yei:-de ရေးတယ်

_____ 5.   like   e. hsei:-yon ဆေးရုံ

_____ 6.   buy   f. a:-ga̩-za: အားကစား

_____ 7.   park   g. pan:-jan ပန်းခြံ

_____ 8.   movie theatre   h. zei: ဈေး

_____ 9.   school   i. ga̩-za:-de ကစားတယ်

_____10.   write   j. ei'-te အိပ်တယ်

_____11.   music   k. jai'-te ကြိုက်တယ်

_____12.   sports   l. nain-de နိုင်တယ်

                                   m. jaun: ကျောင်း

                                   n. ta̩-cho̩ တချို့

                                   o. we-de ဝယ်တယ်

Translate sentences 1-3 into English. Transliterate sentences 4-5 into Burmese.

1. သူ မြန်မာစာ ရေးတတ်တယ်။

_____

2. အိမ်သာကို ရမလဲ။

_____

3. သူ စာအုပ်ဆိုင် သွားချင်တယ်။

_____

4. I am going to the noodle shop.

_____

5. They are at the movie theater.

_____

Complex Vowels

Vowel	Sound	Name
○ငҮ	/o/	lon:-ji:-tin tə-chaun:-ngin လုံးကြီးတင် တစ်ချောင်းငင်
○ဉင	/ain/	lon:-ji:-tin tə-chaun:-ngin ngạ-tha' လုံးကြီးတင် တစ်ချောင်းငင် ငသတ်
○ငက်	/ai'/[20]	lon:-ji:-tin tə-chaun:-ngin kạ-tha' လုံးကြီးတင် တစ်ချောင်းငင် ကသတ်
◌ဲ	/ẹ/	nau'-pyi' au'-kạ-myi' နောက်ပစ် အောက်ကမြစ်
-ယ်	/e/	yạ-tha' ယသတ်
◌ဲ	/e:/	nau'-pyi' နောက်ပစ်
ေ-ာ့	/ɔ̣/	thə-wei-hto: yei:-chạ au'-kạ-myi' သဝေထိုး ရေးချ အောက်ကမြစ်
ေ-ာ်	/ɔ/[21]	thə-wei-hto: yei:-chạ shẹ-hto: သဝေထိုး ရေးချ ရှေ့ ထိုး
ေ-ာ	/ɔ:/	thə-wei-hto: yei:-chạ သဝေထိုး ရေးချ

Notice the last vowel uses a shẹ-hto: to indicate a low tone. In this case, no tone mark (shown below) indicates a high tone.

---

[20] Be careful to note that the /ai/ sound, although very different from /o/, is written the same way except that /ai/ has a kạ-tha' added afterwards.

[21] the symbol used for shẹ-hto: symbol is the same as the ə-tha' symbol, but is called shẹ-hto: when placed above the yei:-chạ.

ေ–ာင် /aun/   thə-wei-hto: yei:-chạ ngạ-tha

သေဝထိုး ေရးချ ငသတ်

ေ–ာက် /au'/   thə-wei-hto: yei:-chạ kạ-tha

သေဝထိုး ေရးချ ကသတ်

Unmarked High Tone

Note that two of the above vowels, nau'-pyi' (`◌̀`) and thə-wei-hto: yei:-chạ (ေ–ာ) are special cases in which a high tone occurs without the wa'-sa-hnə-lon:-bau' (:) character which indicates a high tone mark. Care must be taken to note these vowels and to remember to pronounce their unmarked high tones.

Practice Writing the Following Vowels

Use အ as the consonant when practicing writing the
following vowels. Remember to always start writing a character
with the small circle if there is one.

အယ်	အယ်	အယ်	အယ်
အဲ	အဲ	အဲ	အဲ
အဲ့	အဲ့	အဲ့	အဲ့
အို	အို	အို	အို
အိုင်	အိုင်	အိုင်	အိုင်
အိုက်	အိုက်	အိုက်	အိုက်
အော	အော	အော	အော
အော့	အော့	အော့	အော့
အောင်	အောင်	အောင်	အောင်
အောက်	အောက်	အောက်	အောက်

Read the Following Aloud

1. ကို့   ကို   ကို:

2. ကိုင့်   ကိုင   ကိုင်း   ကိုက်

3. ကဲ့   ကယ်   ကဲ

4. ကော့   ကော်   ကော

5. ကောင့်   ကောင   ကောင်း   ကောက်

6. ခို့   ခို   ခို:

7. ခဲ့   ခယ်   ခဲ

8. ခေါ့   ခေါ်   ခေါ

9. ခေါင့်   ခေါင   ခေါင်း   ခိုက်

10. ခို့   ခို   ခို:

11. ခိုင့်   ခိုင   ခိုင်း   ခိုက်

12. ဂဲ့   ဂယ်   ဂဲ

13. ဂေါ့   ဂေါ်   ဂေါ

14. ဂေါင့်   ဂေါင   ဂေါင်း   ဂိုက်

15. စို့   စို   စို:

16. စိုင့်   စိုင   စိုင်း   စိုက်

17. စဲ့   စယ်   စဲ

18. စော့   စော်   စော

19. စောင့်   စောင   စောင်း   စိုက်

20. ဆို့   ဆို   ဆိုး

21. ဆိုင့်   ဆိုင   ဆိုင်း   ဆိုက်

22. ဆဲ့   ဆယ်   ဆဲ

23. ဆော့   ဆော်   ဆော

24. ဆောင့်   ဆောင   ဆောင်း   ဆိုက်

25. ဇို့   ဇို   ဇို့း

27. ဇဲ့   ဇယ်   ဇဲ

28. ဇော့   ဇော်   ဇော

29. ဇောင့်   ဇောင   ဇောင်း   ဇိုက်

Practice Writing Consonants

Practice writing the following consonants. Remember to use
the proper stroke order as shown below.

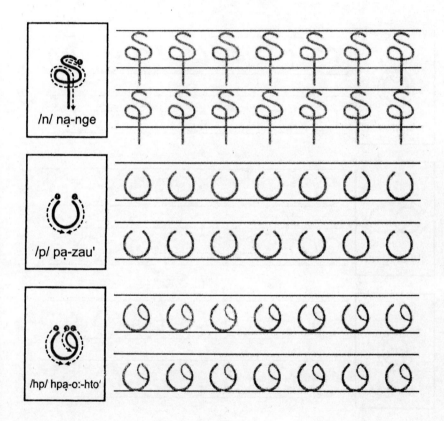

/n/ naౖ-nge

/p/ paౖ-zau'

/hp/ hpaౖ-o:-hto'

Practice Writing Consonants

Practice writing the following consonants. Remember to use the proper stroke order as shown below.

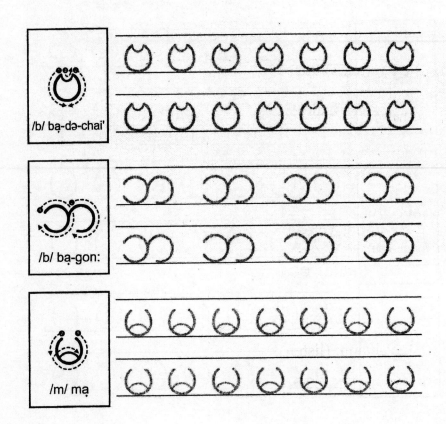

Practice Writing the Following
Words in Myanmar

1. hpan: (catch) ဖမ်း

2. ei' (bag) အိတ်

3. hpo' (bake) ဖုတ်

4. ei'-hkan: (bedroom) အိပ်ခန်း

5. mei:-zi̯ (chin) မေးစေ့

6. ə-tan: (class) အတန်း

7. paun-moṇ (bread)   ပေါင်မုန့်

8. hsau' (build) ဆောက်

9. da-bei-mḛ (but) ဒါပေမဲ့

10. na:-htaun: (listen) နားထောင်

11. pa: (cheek) ပါး

12. tɔ (clever) တော်

13. pei' (cloth) ပိတ်

14. ne' (deep) နက်

15. kai' (ache) ကိုက်

16. pọ-pei: (deliver) ပို့ပေး

17. bei:-zo: (disaster) ဘေးဆိုး

18. mu: (dizzy) မူး

19. maun: (drive) မောင်း

20. di-nẹi (today) ဒီနေ့

21. dɔ (aunt[22]) ဒေါ်

22. a:-ne: (weak) အားနည်း

23. si' (war) စစ်

24. hpə-na' (shoe) ဖိနပ်

25. ə-hsei' (poison) အဆိပ်

---

[22] dɔ is also used as a title for a woman senior to the speaker in age (rather like ma'am in English).

Writing Exercise 3

Write the following words and sounds in Burmese script.

1. nain (can) _____

2. ti-bi (television) _____

3. hpa' (read) _____

4. htə-min: (cooked rice) _____

5. hkɔ (to be called) _____

6. ein (house) _____

7. ə-hte: (inside) _____

8. mei: (ask) _____

9. nau' (next) _____

10. sa-dai' (post office) _____

11. kaun: (good, well) _____

12. sa-o' (book) _____

13. nya̱-nei (evening) _____

14. hke' (difficult) _____

15. mi̱-ni' (minute) _____

16. pan:-jan (park) _____

17. ə-ni (red) _____

18. ə-hti̱ (until) _____

Lesson 4

question words; colors; possessive form; compound verbs; အ prefix and တာ suffix; medial consonants; common consonants IV

thin-gan:-za lei: သင်ခန်းစာ ၄   Lesson 4
wɔ:-ha-ṛa   ဝေါဟာရ   Vocabulary

Nouns

lei'-sa	လိပ်စာ	address
hpon: nan-ba'	ဖုန်း နံပါတ်	phone number
mei'-hswei	မိတ်ဆွေ	acquaintance, friend
thə-nge-jin:	သူငယ်ချင်း	close friend
di-ha	ဒီဟာ	this one
e:-di-ha	အဲဒီဟာ	that one over there
ka:	ကား	car
te'-kə-si	တက္ကစီ	taxi
ba'-sə-ka:	ဘတ်စ်ကား	bus
ka:-gei'	ကားဂိတ်	bus station (lit. "car gate")
lei-yin	လေယာဉ်	airplane[23]
lei-zei'	လေဆိပ်	airport
mi:-yə-hta:	မီးရထား	train
bu-da-yon	ဘူတာရုံ	train station
hsai'-ka:	ဆိုက်ကား	pedicab (lit., "sidecar")
se'-bein:	စက်ဘီး	bicycle
mɔ-tɔ-hsain-ke	မော်တော်ဆိုင်ကယ်	motorcycle
myin:	မြင်း	horse
myin:-hle:	မြင်းလှည်း	horse cart
ə-yaun	အရောင်	color

---

[23] This word includes a special character, nyạ-le:-tha' (ဉ်), an uncommon form of the letter nyạ (ည)

ə-pya	အပြာ	blue[24]
ə-sein:	အစိမ်း	green
ə-wa	အဝါ	yellow
ə-ni	အနီ	red
ə-nyo	အညို	brown
ə-ne', ə-me:	အနက်၊ အမည်း	black
ə-hpyu	အဖြူ	white
be-dhu	ဘယ်သူ	who
da be-dhu ha-le:	ဒါဘယ်သူ့ဟာလဲ။	"Whose is this?"
be-ha...	ဘယ်ဟာ	which one...
be-ha mə-sa'-hpu:-le:		
	ဘယ်ဟာ မစပ်ဘူးလဲ။	"Which one isn't spicy?"
-si:/zi:	စီး	counter for vehicles

Verbs

thi-de	သိတယ်	to know
hma'-mi-de	မှတ်မိတယ်	to recognize
yu-de	ယူတယ်	to take
lan:-shau'-te	လမ်းလျှောက်တယ်	to walk
te'-te	တက်တယ်	to get in/climb up
si:-de	စီးတယ်	to ride
maun:-de	မောင်းတယ်	to drive
ni:-de	နီးတယ်	to be near
wei:-de	ဝေးတယ်	to be far
a:-de	အားတယ်	to be free, unoccupied, have free time

---

[24] note that colors can also be used as verbs, such as ə-pya-de = to be blue.

ma-de	မာတယ်	to be hard
pyɔ̣-de	ပျော့တယ်	to be soft
to-de	တိုတယ်	to be short (length)
she-de	ရှည်တယ်	to be long (length)
tɔ-de	တော်တယ်	to be enough
tɔ-bi	တော်ပြီ။	"that's enough" (used as "I'm full")
ji:-de	ကြီးတယ်	to be big (also a noun particle)
thei:-de	သေးတယ်	to be small
zei:-ji:-de	ဈေးကြီးတယ်	to be expensive
zei:-cho-de	ဈေးချိုတယ်	to be cheap
zei:-mə-cho-bu:	ဈေးမချိုဘူး	not cheap
myan-de	မြန်တယ်	to be fast
hnei:-de	နှေးတယ်	to be slow

Particles

-nẹ	နဲ့	by as in "go by train"
-kạ/gạ	က	from
-ko/go	ကို	to
-yin	ရင်	if

thə-da   သဒ္ဒါ   Grammar

Question Words: Be/Ba

Question words in Burmese are based on two nouns: *be* ဘယ်
(which) and *ba* ဘာ (what). Other question words are formed by
adding a particle to one of these. For example, *where* (be-hma,
ဘယ်မှာ) uses *be* ဘယ် plus the particle *-hma* မှာ. A question
particle le: (လဲ) is then added to the end of the sentence as well.

Where   be-hma...   ဘယ်မှာ
"Where do you live?"   be-hma nei-dhə-le: ဘယ်မှာ နေသလဲ။

If the question is about someone who is going to or coming from
somewhere, the particles -ko/go and -ka̠/ga̠ are used for "where":

"Where will you go to?" be-go thwa:-mə-le: ဘယ်ကို သွားမလဲ။
"Where did you come from?"
                       be-ga̠ la-dhə-le: ဘယ်က လာသလဲ။

Finally, the particle is sometimes left out completely as in the very
informal greeting:

"Where [are you going]?"
                       be-le: ဘယ်လဲ။

Noun Particles: -ko/go ကို and - ka̱/ga̱ ခ

The two forms of "where" are also examples of two common noun particles -ko/go ကို, refering to a place someone is going to and ka̱/ga̱ က, usually translates as meaning from.

He came from the library.
thu sa-ji-dai'-ka̱ la-de.   သူ စာကြည့်တိုက်က လာတယ်။

Sein will go to the market.
sein zei-go thwa:-me.   စိန် ဈေးကို သွားမယ်။

Besides showing destination, -ko/go is also used to indicate the object of a sentence:

[I] met him at school.
thu̱-go jaun:-hma twe̱i-de.   သူ့ကို ကျောင်းမှာ တွေ့တယ်။

[I] like this bicycle.
di se-bein-go jai'-te.   ဒီ စက်ဘီးကို ကြိုက်တယ်။

In this lesson, we will also see ko ကို used in two other ways: as a title, meaning older brother, used to refer to males somewhat older than the speaker, and to indicate that the noun phrase is the object of the sentence rather than the subject (see examples in sentences 1 and 2 in this lesson).

Noun Particle: -yẹ ရဲ့ (Possessive form)

Possession in Burmese can be shown in two ways. First, pronouns can be modified to show possession by adding a creaky tone (‸) to the end:

thụ ein...   သူ့ အိမ်   his/her house...

More generally, possesion is shown by attaching the yẹ (ရဲ့) suffix to a noun:

mạ sein-yẹ ei-hkan: မစိန်ရဲ့ အိပ်ခန်း   Sein's bedroom

Another way to show possession is to use the noun o'-sa ဥစ္စာ meaning property or possession. For example:

e:-di ka: jə-nɔ o'-sa   အဲဒီ ကား ကျွန်တော် ဥစ္စာ။   That car is mine.

Compound Verbs

Two or more verbs can sometimes be used to form a compound verb. For example:

[I] want to go   would be   thwa:-ɉin-de   သွားချင်တယ်။

Verbs used in combination like this include those used to express desire, intention or ability such as:

chin-de	ချင်တယ်	to want
nain-de	နိုင်တယ်	can/able to
yạ-me	ရမယ်	must/ought to

Noun forming particle: a- အ (forms nouns from verbs)

Verbs can be modified to form nouns by adding the letter အ to the beginning of the word. Here's an example with the verb for "to have a fever" hpya: (ဖျား, as in "[I] have a fever", ဖျားတယ်):

အ + ဖျား (verb, have a fever)   =   အဖျား   (noun, fever)

Noun forming particle: -ta တာ (forms nouns from verbs)

A second way of modifying verbs to form nouns is by adding the suffix -ta/da (တာ) to the end of the word. In this case, the meaning is more like "the process of". For example, the verb to speak pyɔ: (ပြော) can be changed to a noun by adding တာ:

ပြော (verb, speak) + တာ   =   ပြောတာ   (noun,
                                                                speaking or speech)

Conversation 1

Aung　yo'-shin thwa:-ji-chin-de.
အောင်　ရုပ်ရှင် သွားကြည့်ချင်တယ်။
I want to go watch a movie.

Sarah　thwa:-jin-de, da-bei-mẹ yo'-shin-yon
　　　di-hma ni:-la:?
စာရာ　သွားချင်တယ်၊ ဒါပေမဲ့ ရုပ်ရှင်ရဲ့ ဒီမှာ နီးလား။
I want to go, but is there a movie theater near here?

Aung　di-lan:-hma yo'-shin-yon-ji: shi̱-de.
အောင်　ဒီလမ်းမှာ ရုပ်ရှင်ရဲ့ကြီး ရှိတယ်။
This street has a big movie theater.

Sarah　yo'-shin-yon wei:-la:?
စာရာ　ရုပ်ရှင်ရဲ့ ဝေးလား။
Is the theater far?

Aung　mə-wei:-bu:. thwa:-jin-dhə-la:?
အောင်　မဝေးဘူး။ သွားချင်သလား။
It's not far. Do [you] want to go?

Sarah　ho'-kẹ, thwa:-jin-de.
စာရာ　ဟုတ်ကဲ့၊ သွားချင်တယ်။
Yes, [I] want to go.

Conversation 2

Joe   nyi-lei:[25], nyi-lei: te'-kə-si a:-la:?
ဂျိုး   ညီလေး၊ ညီလေး တက္ကစီ အားလား။
                        Sir, sir is your taxi free?

Taxi Driver: be thwa:-mə-le:?
တက္ကစီ မောင်းတယ် ဘယ် သွားမလဲ။
                        Where are you going?

Joe   aun-min-gə-la ka:-gei' thwa:-jin-de.
ဂျိုး   အောင်မင်္ဂလာ ကားဂိတ် သွားချင်တယ်။
                        I want to go to Aungmingalar bus station.

Taxi Driver: o, a-yan: wei:-de.
မောင်းတယ်   အို၊ အရမ်း ဝေးတယ်။
                        oh, that's so far.

Joe   e:-di-go thwa:-yin be lau'-le:?
ဂျိုး   အဲဒီကို သွားရင် ဘယ် လောက်လဲ။
                        If [we] go there, how much?

Taxi Driver: nga:-daun nga:-ya-ba.
မောင်းတယ်   ငါးထောင့် ငါးရာပါ။
                        Five thousand five hundred, sir.

---

[25] Nyi-lei: literally means younger brother. U:-lei: (uncle, ဦးလေး) is used to
address an older man.

wa-ja̱-mya: ဝါကျများ:   **Sentences**

1.   A: thu̱-go thi̱-la:?
          သူ့ကို သိလား။
          Do you know him?

     B: thi̱-de.
          သိတယ်။
          I know him.

     C: thu̱-go mə-thi̱-bu:.
          သူ့ကို မသိဘူး။
          I don't know him.

2.   A: be-dhu̱-go thi̱-dhə-le:.
          ဘယ်သူ့ကို သိသလဲ။
          Who do you know?

     B: ko-zɔ ko-win:-ne̱ ko-min:-go thi̱-de.
          ကိုဇော် ကိုဝင်းနဲ့ ကိုမင်းကို သိတယ်။
          I know Ko Zaw, Ko Win and Ko Min.

3.   A: jə-nɔ hpon:-nan-ba' thi̱-la:?
          ကျွန်တော့် ဖုန်းနံပါတ် သိလား။
          Do you know my phone number?

     B: ho'-ke̱, thi̱-de.
          ဟုတ်ကဲ့၊ သိတယ်။
          Yes, [I] know [it].

4.   A: be-ga̱ la-dhə-le:?
          ဘယ်က လာသလဲ။
          Where does she come from?

B: mə-thi̞-bu:.

မသိဘူး။

I don't know.

C: yan-gon-ga̞ la-de.

ရန်ကုန်က လာတယ်။

She comes from Yangon.

A: ka: be-hnə-si: shi̞-dhə-le:?

ကား ဘယ်နှစ်စီး ရှိသလဲ။

How many cars do [you] have?

B: ka: hnə-si: shi̞-de.

ကား နှစ်စီး ရှိတယ်။

[I] have two cars.

A: be-hnə-dɔ-la shi̞-dhə-le:?

ဘယ်နှစ်ဒေါ်လာ ရှိသလဲ။

How many dollars do you have?

B: thon:-dɔ-la shi̞-de.

သုံးဒေါ်လာ ရှိတယ်။

I have three dollars.

A: bə-ma-zə-ga: thin-da be-hnə-hni' shi̞-bi-le:?

ဗမာစကား သင်တာ ဘယ်နှစ်နှစ် ရှိပြီလဲ။

How many years have you been studying Burmese?

B: bə-ma-zə-ga: thin-da tə-la̞ shi̞-bi.

မြန်မာစကား သင်တာ တစ်လ ရှိပြီ။

I've been studying Burmese for one month.

8. thu in:-gə-lei'-sə-ga: ne:-ne: pyɔ:-da'-te.
သူ အင်္ဂလိပ်စကား နည်းနည်း ပြောတတ်တယ်။
He can speak a little English.

9. thu̥-hma pai'-hsan ə-mya:-ɟi: shi̥-de.
သူ့မှာ ပိုက်ဆံ အများကြီး ရှိတယ်။
He has a lot of money.

10. e:-di ein ɟi:-de.
အဲဒီ အိမ် ကြီးတယ်။
That is a big house!

11. thu bə-ma-lo ə-mya:-ɟi: thi̥-de.
သူ ဗမာလို အများကြီး သိတယ်။
She knows a lot of Burmese!

12. A: be-lau' yu-mə-le:?
ဘယ်လောက် ယူမလဲ။
How much will you take?

B: ne:-ne:-ba-be.
နည်းနည်းပါပဲ။
Just a little bit, please.

13. hsain-go thwa:-pi:-bi.
ဆိုင်ကို သွားပြီးပြီ။
I went to the store already.

14. thu̥-hma ka: we-pi:-bi.
သူ့မှာ ကား ဝယ်ပြီးပြီ။
He already bought a car.

15. A: thu̥ ein wei:-de.
သူ့ အိမ် ဝေးတယ်။
His house is far.

B: thụ ein ni:-de.
      သူ့ အိမ် နီးတယ်॥
      His house is near.

16.   A: di ei'-ya thei' ma-de.
            ဒီ အိပ်ရာ သိပ် မာတယ်॥
            This bed is very hard.

      B: di ei'-ya thei' pyɔ̣-de.
            ဒီ အိပ်ရာ သိပ် ပျော့တယ်॥
            This bed is very soft.

17.   A: da ə-yan: to-de.
            ဒါ အရမ်း တိုတယ်॥
            This one is too short.

      B: da ə-yan: ji:-de.
            ဒါ အရမ်း ကြီးတယ်॥
            This one is too big.

18.   di ka: thei' myan-de. da-bei-mẹ mə-we-jin-bu:.
            ဒီ ကား သိပ် မြန်တယ်॥ ဒါပေမဲ့ မဝယ်ချင်ဘူး॥
            This car is very fast. But I don't want to buy it.

19.   mei'-hswei-nẹ lan:-shau'-chin-de.
            မိတ်ဆွေနဲ့ လမ်းလျှောက်ချင်တယ်॥
            I want to walk with [my] friend.

20.   di sa:-thau'-hsain kaun:-de. ho-hma sa:-jin-de.
            ဒီ စားသောက်ဆိုင် ကောင်းတယ်॥ ဟိုမှာ
            စားချင်တယ်॥
            This restaurant is good. I want to eat there.

Drills

1. Practice writing the following sentences in Burmese. If it is a question, practice answering the question as well.

What color do you like?

_____

Do you want to go and eat at the market?

_____

I want to go to the airport.

_____

2. Do at least one of the following:

Write a two person dialog describing how much something is and if it is cheap or expensive.

Write a paragraph describing something. Use at least three particles.

Write six sentences using ta'-te, thi-de and hma-mi-de (three verbs for "to know").

3. Use the following words to help form ten sentences.

lan: လမ်း   yu-de ယူတယ်   lan:-shau'
                                                 လမ်းလျှောက်

lei'-sa လိပ်စာ   ji. ကြည့်   zei:-cho-de
                                                 ဈေးချိုတယ်

mei'-hswei မိတ်ဆွေ   ə-mya: အများ   zei:-ji:-de
                                                 ဈေးကြီးတယ်

thei' သိပ်   tə-bi တော်ပြီ   ka: ကား

myan မြန်   hnei: နှေး   be-lau'-le:
                                                 ဘယ်လောက်လဲ

thei: သေး   ka: ကား   ni: နီး

si:-de စီးတယ်   wei: ဝေး   ə-pya အပြာ

myin: မြင်း   ə-sein: အစိမ်း   ə-ni အနီ

ə-ne' အနက်   ə-hpyu အဖြူ   be-ha-le:
                                                 ဘယ်ဟာလဲ

Test 4

Match the English words with the Burmese words.

_____ 1. friend

_____ 2. difficult

_____ 3. green

_____ 4. far

_____ 5. car

_____ 6. near

_____ 7. soft

_____ 8. know

_____ 9. address

_____10. to be red

_____11. many

_____12. cheap

_____13. it's big

_____14. enough

a. ji:-de ကြီးတယ်

b. lei'-sa လိပ်စာ

c. ə-mya: အများ

d. pyɔ့ ပျော့

e. wei: ဝေး

f. ə-sein: အစိမ်း

g. ni-de နီတယ်

h. thei: သေး

i. zei:-cho-de ဈေးချိုတယ်

j. ka: ကား

k. tɔ-bi တော်ပြီ

l. hke' ခက်

m. mei'-hswei မိတ်ဆွေ

n. zei:-ji:-de ဈေးကြီးတယ်

o. thị-de သိတယ်

p. thei' သိပ်

q. ni: နီး

Translate sentences 1-3 into English. Transliterate sentences 4-5 into Burmese.

1. ကား ဘယ်နှစ်စီး ရှိသလဲ။

2. ဆိုင်ကို မသွားချင်ဘူး။ အရမ်း ဝေးတယ်။

3. ဘုရား သွားရင် ဘယ်လောက်လဲ။

4. Is this taxi free?

5. That’s expensive. Will you take 3500 kyats?

Word Exercise

Insert the correct form of the word 'to know' (thi̱-de, ta'-te, or hma'-mi-de) in the following sentences.

1. သူ နာမည် _____။
    thu na-me _____.
    [I] (know) his name.

2. သူ တရုတ်စကား ပြော _____။
    thu tə-yo'-sə-ga: pyɔ: _____.
    She (knows) how to speak Chinese.

3. သူ ကျွန်တော့် အိမ် _____။
    thu jə-nɔ̱ ein _____.
    She knows (recognizes) my house.

4. လေဆိပ်ကို သွား _____။
    lei-zei'-ko thwa: _____.
    I (know) how to go to the airport.

5. ဟုတ်ကဲ့ မနန္ဒာ _____ . သူ ကျွန်မရဲ့ မိတ်ဆွေ။
    ho'-kẹ, ma-nan-da _____ . thu jə-mạ-yẹ mei'-hswe.
    Yes, I (know) Nanda. She is my friend.

Medial Consonants

Consonant	Name	Pronunciation
၂	yạ-piṇ	/medial 'y' sound/
ြ	yạ-yi'	/medial 'y' sound/
ြ	yạ-yi'	/medial 'y' sound/ (used for wider consonants)
◌ွ	wạ-hswe:	/medial 'w' sound/

Burmese has three medial consonants, shown above. The first two, yạ-piṇ and yạ-yi' produce a "y" sound, while the third, wạ-hswe: represents a medial "w" sound. There are exceptions, however, and so in some words the medial sound is reduced or even absent. Also note that when either yạ-piṇ or yạ-yi' is combined with kạ-ji:, hkạ-gwe or gạ-nge it does not represent a medial "y" sounds but the j, j̲ and ch sounds, respectively. Medial consonants can also be combined with other symbols as follows:

Consonant	Name	Pronunciation
ချ	ya̦-pin̦ wa̦-hswe:	/medial y + w sounds/
ဂျ	ya̦-pin̦ ha̦-hto:	/medial y plus aspiration/
ခွ	wa̦-hswe: ha̦-hto:	/medial w plus aspiration/

Practice Writing the Following Words

Practicing writing the these examples of medial consonants. Start writing a character with the small circle if there is one.

ya̦-pin̦ - ျ

chin (want) ချင်

ə-mya: (many, a lot) အများ:

jaun: (school) ကျောင်း

tə-cho̧ (some) တချို့

che' (cook) ချက်

jɔ: (back) ကျော

jə-pan (Japan) ဂျပန်

yạ-yi' - ြ

ji: (big) ကြီး

pyɔ: (speak) ပြော

jai' (like) ကြိုက်

myọ (city) မြို့

myan-ma (Myanmar) မြန်မာ

pye (country) ပြည်

je' (chicken) ကြက်

myan-myan (quick, hurry!) မြန်မြန်

wạ-hswe - ဝ

zun: (spoon) ဇွန်း

nwei: (warm) နွေး

pwe: (festival) ပွဲ

thwa: (go) သွား

hkwei: (dog) ခွေး

thwei: (blood) သွေး

lwe (easy) လွယ်

Practice Writing Consonants

Practice writing the following consonants. Remember to use the proper stroke order as shown below.

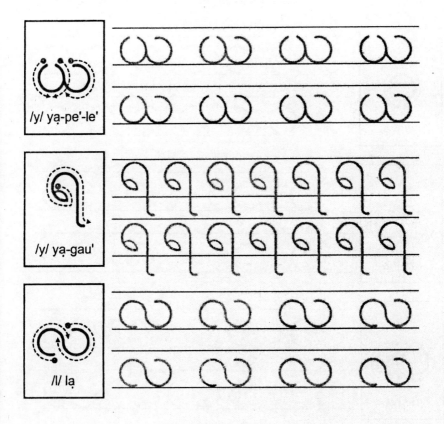

Practice Writing Consonants

Practice writing the following consonants. Remember to use the proper stroke order as shown below.

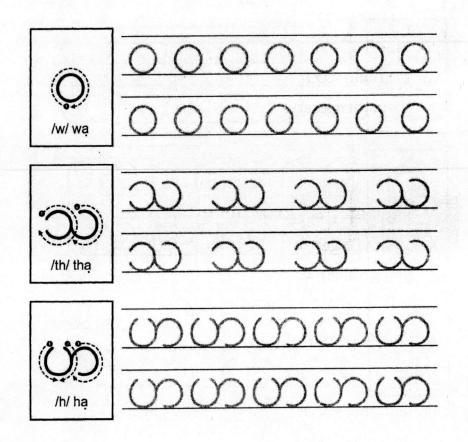

Practice Writing the Following Words in Myanmar

yạ-pe'-le' ယ

1. yu (take) ယူ
2. yin (fly) ယင်
3. ya: (itch) ယား
4. ya-yi (temporary) ယာယီ
5. yau' (classifier for people) ယောက်

yạ-gau' ရ

6. yei (water) ရေ
7. ywa (village) ရွာ
8. yon: (office) ရုံး
9. yi' (pheasant) ရစ်
10. yi:-za: (lover, boy/girlfriend) ရည်းစား

lạ လ

11. lei: (four) လေး
12. la (come) လာ
13. le' (hand, arm) လက်
14. la'-hpe'-ye (tea) လက်ဖက်ရည်
15. lei-zei' (airport) လေဆိပ်

wạ ၀

16. wei: (far) ဝေး

17. we' (pig) ဝက်

18. win (enter) ဝင်

19. we (buy) ဝယ်

20. wạ-de (fat) ၀တယ်

thạ သ

21. thə-mi: (daughter) သမီး

22. tha: (son) သား

23. thau' (drink) သောက်

24. thin-de (study) သင်တယ်

25. thei' (very) သိပ်

hạ ဟ

26. ho (there) ဟို

27. ho'-kẹ (yes) ဟုတ်ကဲ့

28. he:-lo (hello) ဟဲလို

29. hin: (curry) ဟင်း

30. ho-te (hotel) ဟိုတယ်

R words using yạ-gau' (ရ)

Yạ-gau' was originally used to indicate an "r" sound but is now generally used for a "y" sound. Some foreign borrow words still exist, however, along with some Pali words that use yạ-gau'. Examples of these include the following:

Animal	တိရစ္ဆာန်	tə-**rei**'-hsan (from Pali)
Camera	ကင်မရာ	kin-mə-**ra**
Radio	ရေဒီယို	**rei**-di-yo
Rubber	ရော်ဘာ	**r**ɔ-ba
Tourist	တူးရစ်	tu:-**ri**'

Yạ-gau' is also still pronounced as an "r" in the Rakhine dialect of Burmese and was likely the source for the former pronunciation of Yangon as "Rangoon" (ရန်ကုန်).

Writing Exercise 4

Write the following words and sounds in Burmese script.

1. lan: (road)   _____

2. ein-dha (bathroom)   _____

3. di-ha (this one)   _____

4. wei: (far)   _____

5. ə-wa (yellow)   _____

6. da'-pon (photo)   _____

7. mye'-hman (eyeglasses)   _____

8. te-li-hpon: (telephone)   _____

9. thin-de (to study)   _____

10. lwe (easy)   _____

11. ya̰-ba-de (that's all right)   _____

12. hnei: (slow)   _____

13. ho-te (to ride)   _____

14. sa:-thau'-hsain (restaurant)   _____

15. lei'-sa (address)   _____

16. ho'-kḛ (yes)   _____

17. myan-ma-za (written Burmese)   _____

18. thwa:-de (go)   _____

Lesson 5

telling time; day structure; time terms; days of the week; writing Burmese numbers; aspiration; final consonant symbols

thin-gan:-za nga: သင်ခန်းစာ ၅   Lesson 5
wɔ:-ha-ra̩   ဝေါဟာရ   Vocabulary

Nouns

ə-chein	အချိန်	time
mə-ne'	မနက်	morning
nei̩-le	နေ့လည်	afternoon
nya̩-nei	ညနေ	evening
nya̩	ည	night
-pain:	ပိုင်း	suffix indicating period of time
mə-ne'-pain:	မနက်ပိုင်း	during the morning
di-nya̩	ဒီည	tonight
dhə-gaun	သန်းခေါင်	midnight
na-yi	နာရီ	hour
mi̩-ni'	မိနစ်	minute
se'-kan̩	စက္ကန့်	second
hkwe:	ခွဲ	half
na-yi-we'	နာရီဝက်	half an hour
gə-de:-ga̩	ကတည်းက	since
ə-tu-du	အတူတူ	together
nau'	နောက်	after, later
nau'-pi:	နောက်ပြီး	then, after that
nei̩	နေ့	day
di-nei̩	ဒီနေ့	today
-ye'	ရက်	counting word for days
hnə-ye'	နှစ်ရက်	two days

tə-cha:	တခြား	other, another
tə-cha:-ye'	တခြားရက်	another day
a:-la'-ye'	အားလပ်ရက်	holiday; day off
mə-ne'-hpyan	မနက်ဖြန်	tomorrow
dhə-be'-hka	သန်ဘက်ခါ	day after tomorrow
mə-nei̇̀-gạ	မနေ့က	yesterday
tə-nei̇̀-gạ	တနေ့က	day before yesterday
be-don:-gạ	ဘယ်တုန်းက	when (in the past)
be-dɔ̣	ဘယ်တော့	when (in the future)
mə-tain-mi	မတိုင်မီ	before

Verbs

sin:-za:-de	စဉ်းစားတယ်	to think
yau'-te	ရောက်တယ်	to arrive
twei̇̀-de	တွေ့တယ်	to meet
ku-nyi-de	ကူညီတယ်	to help
ku-nyi-ba!	ကူညီပါ။	Help!
sạ-de	စတယ်	to start, begin
hsin:-de	ဆင်းတယ်	to get out (of school, work, etc.)
pi:-de	ပြီးတယ်	to finish, end
ə-lo'-mya:-de	အလုပ်များတယ်	to be busy
hse'-	ဆက်	go on, carry on, keep on (adv)

ə-chein   အချိန်   **Time**

What time is it?

Two phrases are commonly used in Burmese for "what time is it?":
1. What time is it? be-ə-chein shị-bi-le: ဘယ်အချိန် ရှိပြီလဲ။
2. What hour is it? be-hnə-na-yi shị-bi-le: ဘယ်နှစ်နာရီ ရှိပြီလဲ။

Time: Day Structure.

The Burmese day is broken into four parts as follows:
- mə-ne' မနက် ("morning" from 4 to 11 a.m.)
- nej-le or nej-gin:, နေ့လယ်၊ နေ့ခင်း ("afternoon" from 12 to 3 p.m.)
- nyạ-nei, ညနေ ("evening", from about 3 to 7 p.m.)
- nyạ ည (night, between 7 p.m. and before 4 a.m.)

Time: Hours of the Day

mə-ne' lei:-na-yi	မနက် လေးနာရီ	4:00 a.m.
mə-ne' nga:-na-yi	မနက် ငါးနာရီ	5:00 a.m.
mə-ne' chau'-na-yi	မနက် ခြောက်နာရီ	6:00 a.m.
mə-ne' hkun-hnə-na-yi	မနက် ခုနှစ်နာရီ	7:00 a.m.
mə-ne' shi'-na-yi	မနက် ရှစ်နာရီ	8:00 a.m.

mə-ne' ko:-na-yi	မနက် ကိုးနာရီ	9:00 a.m.
mə-ne' hse-na-yi	မနက် ဆယ်နာရီ	10:00 a.m.
mə-ne' hsẹ-tə'-na-yi	မနက် ဆယ့်တစ်နာရီ	11:00 a.m.
mun:-dẹ	မွန်းတည့်	Noon
neị-le tə-na-yi	နေ့လည် တစ်နာရီ	1:00 p.m.
neị-le hnə-na-yi	နေ့လည် နှစ်နာရီ	2:00 p.m.
nyạ-nei thon:-na-yi	ညနေ သုံးနာရီ	3:00 p.m.
nyạ-nei lei:-na-yi	ညနေ လေးနာရီ	4:00 p.m
nyạ-nei nga:-na-yi	ညနေ ငါးနာရီ	5:00 p.m.
nyạ-nei chau'-na-yi	ညနေ ခြောက်နာရီ	6:00 p.m.
nyạ hkun-hnə-na-yi	ည ခုနှစ်နာရီ	7:00 p.m.
nyạ shi'-na-yi	ည ရှစ်နာရီ	8:00 p.m.
nyạ ko:-na-yi	ည ကိုးနာရီ	9:00 p.m.
nyạ hse-na-yi	ည ဆယ်နာရီ	10:00 p.m.
nyạ hsẹ-tə-na-yi	ည ဆယ့်တစ်နာရီ	11:00 p.m.
dhə-gaun	သန်းခေါင်	Midnight
nyạ tə-na-yi	ည တစ်နာရီ	1:00 a.m.
nyạ hnə-na-yi	ည နှစ်နာရီ	2:00 a.m.
nyạ thon:-na-yi	ည သုံးနာရီ	3:00 a.m.

Conversation 1

Thet	di-nẹ be thwa:-mə-le:?
သက်	ဒီနေ့ ဘယ် သွားမလဲ။

Where are you going today?

Bill	O di-nẹ ə-lo'-mya:-de. mə-ne' jaun: thwa:-me.
	nau'-pi: neị-gin: zei: thwa:-me.
ဘီလ်	အို ဒီနေ့ အလုပ်များတယ်။ မနက် ကျောင်း
	သွားမယ်။ နောက်ပြီး နေ့ခင်း ဈေး သွားမယ်။

Oh, I'm busy today .

This morning I'm going to school.

Then, this afternoon I am going to the market.

Thet	zei: be-hnə-na-yi thwa:-mə-le:?
သက်	ဈေး ဘယ်နှစ်နာရီ သွားမလဲ။

What time are you going to the market?

Drills

1. Translate and say the following sentences in Myanmar. Some sentences can be said in different ways. If the sentence is a question, practice answering it too.

When did you get here?

_____

When are you going to Myanmar?

_____

Class starts at 7:00 in the morning.

_____

I am going to play sports with my friends.

_____

Conversation 2

Hein
ဟိန်း
ba lo'-nei-dhə-le:?
ဘာ လုပ်နေသလဲ။
What are you doing?

John
ရွှန်
myan-ma-lo thin-nei-de. hnə-na-yi thin-pi:-bi.
မြန်မာလို သင်နေတယ်။ နှစ်နာရီ သင်ပြီးပြီ။
I am studying Myanmar.
I've been studying for two hours already.

Hein
ဟိန်း
myan-ma-zə-ga: ə-yan: hke'-thə-la:?
မြန်မာစကား အရမ်း ခက်သလား။
Is Myanmar very difficult?

John
ရွှန်
ho'-ke, hke'-te. ku-nyi-lọ yạ-mə-la:?
ဟုတ်ကဲ့၊ ခက်တယ်။ ကူညီလို့ ရမလား။
Yes, it's difficult. Can you help with it?

Hein
ဟိန်း
ku-nyi-lọ yạ-de. da-bei-mẹ nga:-na-yi-hma
mei'-hswei-go thwa:-twei̭-yạ-me.
ကူညီလို့ ရတယ်။ ဒါပေမဲ့ ငါး နာရီမှာ
မိတ်ဆွေကို သွားတွေ့ရမယ်။
I can help, but I must go meet a friend at five
o'clock.

wa-ja̱-mya: ဝါကျများ:   **Sentences**

1.   A: be-ə-chein thin-da jai'-thə-le:?

ဘယ်အချိန် သင်တာ ကြိုက်သလဲ။

What time of day do you like to study?

      B: mə-ne'-pain: thin-da jai'-te.

မနက်ပိုင်း သင်တာ ကြိုက်တယ်။

I like to study in the morning.

      C: nya̱-bain: thin-da jai'-te.

ညပိုင်း သင်တာ ကြိုက်တယ်။

I like to study at night.

      D: nya̱-nei-bain: thin-da jai'-te.

ညနေပိုင်း သင်တာ ကြိုက်တယ်။

I like to study in the evening.

2.   A: jaun: be-ə-chein sa̱-le:?

ကျောင်း ဘယ်အချိန် စလဲ။

What time does school start?

      B: jaun: mə-ne' shi'-na-yi-hma sa̱-de.

ကျောင်း မနက် ရှစ်နာရီမှာ စတယ်။

School starts at eight in the morning.

      C: jaun:-go hkun-hnə-na-yi-hkwe: thwa:-de.

ကျောင်းကို ခုနစ်နာရီခွဲ သွားတယ်။

I go to school at half past seven.

3.   A: jaun: be-ə-chein hsin:-dhə-le:?

ကျောင်း ဘယ်အချိန် ဆင်းသလဲ။

What time is school over?

B: jaun: nyạ-nei thon:-na-yi hsin:-de.

ကျောင်း ညနေ သုံးနာရီ ဆင်းတယ်။

School gets out at three in the evening[26].

C: yo'-shin hkun-hnə-na-yi-hma sạ-de.

ရုပ်ရှင် ခုနှစ်နာရီမှာ စတယ်။

The movie starts at seven.

4.   A: be-ə-chein yau'-le:?

ဘယ်အချိန် ရောက်လဲ။

What time did you get here?

B: nyạ-nei nga:-na-yi gə-de:-gạ shị-nei-de.

ညနေ ငါးနာရီ ကတည်းက ရှိနေတယ်။

[I] have been here since five in the evening.

C: di-hma mə-ne' lei:-na-yi gə-de:-gạ shị-nei-de.

ဒီမှာ မနက် လေးနာရီ ကတည်းက ရှိနေတယ်။

[I] have been here since four in the morning.

5.   A: yan-gon-go be-ə-chein thwa:-jin-le:?

ရန်ကုန်ကို ဘယ်အချိန် သွားချင်လဲ။

What time do you want to go to Yangon?

---

[26] 3 p.m. is considered the start of the evening in Myanmar.

B: yan-gon-go di-nyạ thwa:-jin-de.
      ရန်ကုန်ကို ဒီည သွားချင်တယ်။
      I want to go to Yangon tonight.

6.   A: zei:-hma yau'-ta be-hnə-na-yi shị-bi-le:?
            ဈေးမှာ ရောက်တာ ဘယ်နှစ်နာရီ ရှိပြီလဲ။
            How many hours have you been at the market?

      B: zei:-hma yau'-ta hnə-na-yi shị-bi.
            ဈေးမှာ ရောက်တာ နှစ်နာရီ ရှိပြီ။
            I have been at the market for two hours.

      C: zei:-hma yau'-ta na-yi-we' shị-bi.
            ဈေးမှာ ရောက်တာ နာရီဝက် ရှိပြီ။
            I have been at the market for half an hour.

      D: zei:-hma yau'-ta hse mị-ni' shị-bi.
            ဈေးမှာ ရောက်တာ ဆယ် မိနစ် ရှိပြီ။
            I have been at the market for ten minutes.

7.   A: nau'-be-hnə-na-yi hse'-lo'-mə-le:?
            နောက်ဘယ်နှစ်နာရီ ဆက်လုပ်မလဲ။
            How much longer do you want to work?

      B: nau'-hnə-na-yi hse'-lo'-chin-de.
            နောက်နှစ်နာရီ ဆက်လုပ်ချင်တယ်။
            I want to work for two more hours.

C: nau'-tə-na-yi-hkwe: hse'-lo'-chin-de.

 နောက်တစ်နာရီခွဲ ဆက်လုပ်ချင်တယ်॥

I want to keep working for one and a half more hours.

D: nau'-hse̞-nga: mi̞-ni'-lau' hse'-lo'-me.

နောက်ဆယ့်ငါး မိနစ်လောက် ဆက်လုပ်မယ်॥

I will keep working for about fifteen more minutes.

E: hse'-mə-lo'-chin-hpu:.

ဆက်မလုပ်ချင်ဘူး॥

I don't want to work any more.

8.   A: myan-ma-nain-gan-go be-dhu-ne̞ thwa:-mə-le:?

မြန်မာနိုင်ငံကို ဘယ်သူနဲ့ သွားမလဲ॥

Who do you want to go to Myanmar with?

B: myan-ma-nain-gan-go mei'-hswei-ne̞ thwa:-me.

မြန်မာနိုင်ငံကို မိတ်ဆွေနဲ့ သွားမယ်॥

I want to go to Myanmar with friends.

Drills

1. Translate and say the following sentences in Myanmar. Some sentences can be said in different ways. If the sentence is a question, practice answering it too.

When did you get here?

_____

When are you going to Myanmar?

_____

Class starts at 7:00 in the morning.

_____

I am going to play sports with my friends.

_____

2. Do one of the following.

Create a two person dialogue about a certain activity and what time it will take place. The dialogue must have at least two parts for each participant.

Notice where you are. Tell someone in Myanmar how long you have been at that place. Tell them in two different ways.

3. Use the following words to form ten sentences.

pi:-de ပြီးတယ်	ti' တစ်	sa-de စတယ်
na-yi နာရီ	jaun: ကျောင်း	be-lau'-le: ဘယ်လောက်လဲ
jə-ma ကျွန်မ	ə-the' အသက်	gə-de:-ga ကတည်းက
be-dɔ ဘယ်တော့	e:-da အဲဒါ	shi' ရှိ
-hma မှာ	ə-chein အချိန်	jai'-te ကြိုက်တယ်
mə-ne' မနက်	nei-le နေ့လည်	a-lo'-lo'-te အလုပ်လုပ်တယ်
-pain ပိုင်း	hkwe: ခွဲ	na:-htaun-de နားထောင်တယ်
mi-ni' မိနစ်	thwa:-de သွား	chau'-hse ခြောက်ဆယ်
ji-de ကြည့်တယ်	-nə နဲ့	nya-nei ညနေ
-le: လည်း	twei-de တွေ့တယ်	la-de လာတယ်
-ko/go ကို	nya ည	yau'-te ရောက်တယ်

Test 5

Write these times in Burmese.

1. 4:00 am _____

2. 6:00 pm _____

3. 12:00 am _____

4. 3:50 pm _____

5. 11:30 am _____

6. 10:45 pm _____

7. 5:05 pm _____

Write these times in English. For each time make sure to specify a.m. or p.m.

1. nya-nei hkun-hnə-na-yi   _____

2. mə-ne' thon:-na-yi   _____

3. mə-ne' chau'-na-yi   _____

4. nei-le hnə-na-yi lei:-zẹ-lei: mị-ni'   _____

5. mə-ne' hse-na-yi hnə-hsẹ-nga: mị-ni'   _____

6. nei-le   _____

7. nya-nei lei:-na-yi   _____

Translate sentences 1-3 into English. Transliterate sentences 4-6 into Burmese.

1. သုံးနာရီလောက် ရောက်မယ်။

_____

2. အလုပ်ကို မနက် ငါးနာရီ သွားတယ်။

_____

3. မနက်ပိုင်း သူ အိပ်ချင်တယ်။

_____

4. Bill's school gets out at 4:00 pm.

_____

5. [I] already read that book.

_____

6. Will you follow me to the movie theater?

_____

Practice Writing Consonants

Practice writing the following consonants. Remember to use the proper stroke order as shown below.

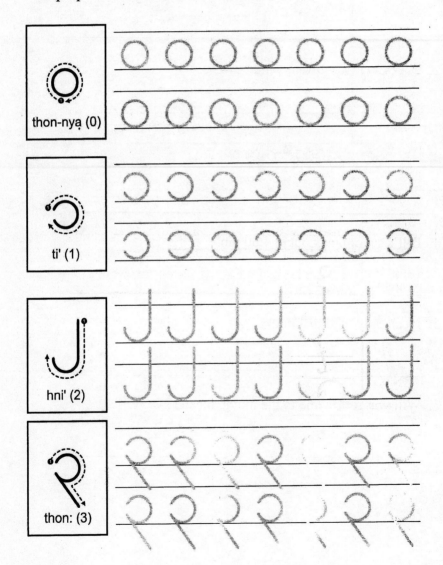

thon-nyạ (0)	
ti' (1)	
hni' (2)	
thon: (3)	

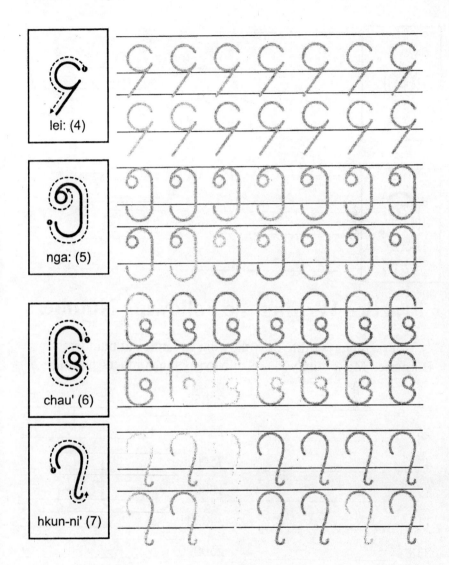

lei: (4)

nga: (5)

chau' (6)

hkun-ni' (7)

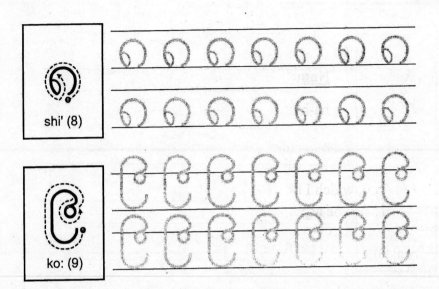

shi' (8)

ko: (9)

Practice Writing the Following Numbers

Practicing writing the following examples of numbers in Burmese. Make sure you are able to say the numbers as well.

15	_____	2005	_____
26	_____	2344	_____
47	_____	7590	_____
89	_____	16000	_____
113	_____	34922	_____
238	_____	250000	_____
577	_____	767000	_____
1550	_____	1430000	_____
1997	_____	5000000	_____

Aspiration

Symbol	Name	Pronunciation
⸜	ha-hto:	/marks aspiration/

A number of "second column" letters in the Burmese alphabet are aspirated consonants, such as hka-gwe (ə), hsa-lein (ဆ), and hta-hsin-du (ထ), which I have already introduced. Several other consonants can be aspirated, indicated by the addition of the ha-hto: mark shown above. The most commonly aspirated consonants that use ha-hto: are ma (ဟ) and na-nge (ၡ). Also the letter ya-gau' (ၡ) uses ha-hto: for the "sh" sound in Burmese.

Practice Writing the Following Words

Practicing writing the following examples of words in which the consonants mark their aspiration using the ha-hto: symbol.

ha-hto: ⸜

hnge' (bird) ငှက်

hnga: (borrow, hire or rent) ငှား

hni' (year) နှစ်

hnei: (slow) နှေး

di-hma (here) ဒီမှာ

hla (pretty) လှ

hli: (slice, peel) လှီး

shin (you, female speaker) ရှင်

shi (to be) ရှိ

hwe' (hide, conceal) ဝှက်

Consonant-Vowel Combinations Using hạ-hto:

〒   hạ-hto: tə-chaun:-ngin   /ụ sound plus aspiration/
JL

〒   hạ-hto: hnə-chaun:-ngin   /u sound plus aspiration/
JL

Final Consonant Symbols

Symbol   **Name**

°
−   / final n sound/   thei:-dhei:-tin (same as $\displaystyle \frac{c}{3}$ or ﻬ)

ε
−   /final n sound/   kin:-zi: (same as ̃C)

Thei:-dhei:-tin is an alternate way of writing the final n consonant
and is sometimes used instead of nạ-tha' (§) or mạ-tha' (ﻬ). kin:-
zi: is an alternate form of ngạ-tha' (̃C).

Practice Writing the Following Words

Practicing writing the following examples of words in which the consonants mark their aspiration using the thei:-dhei:-tin and kin:-zi: symbols.

thei:-dhei:-tin ̊ -

thon: (three) သုံး   zə-bin (hair (on the head)) ဆံပင်

pə-hkon: (shoulder) ပခုံး   wun-bə-lwei (wolf) ဝံပုလွေ

də'-pon (photograph) ဓာတ်ပုံ   than-yon: (embassy) သံရုံး

hke:-dan (pencil) ခဲတံ   nan-ba' (number) နံပါတ်

kin:-zi: ̣ -

thin:-bɔ: (ship) သင်္ဘော

tə-nin:-la-neị (Monday) တနင်္လာနေ့

in-ga-neị (Tuesday) အင်္ဂါနေ့

in:-gə-leị' (English) အင်္ဂလိပ်

Writing Exercise 5

Write the following numbers using the Burmese numbers.

1. 123	_____	2. 676	_____
3. 590	_____	4. 2084	_____
5. 3561	_____	6. 1873	_____
7. 2492	_____	8. 5637	_____

Write the following using Burmese script (including numbers).

9. in-ga-neị mə-ne' (Tuesday morning) _____

10. pyin-dhi'-lu-myo: (French person) _____

11. ba'-sə-ka: nan-ba' lei:-zẹ-nga: (bus number 45) _____

12. da'-pon yai'-mə-la:? (Can [I] take a photo?)_____

13. di-go la-ba, shin. (Please come here, sir) _____

14. hni' ko: lei: pan:-so:dan: lan:. (294 Pansodan Street)

_____

15. mi:-yə-hta: chau'-na-yi yau'-te. (The train arrives at six o'clock)

_____

16. di-nei. pan:-jan thwa:-me. (Today [I] will go to the park.)

_____

17. in:-ga-lei'-sə-ga: pyɔ:-da'-la:? (Can you speak English?)

_____

18. di-lan:-hma htain:-than-yon: shi-de. (The Thai embassy is on this street) _____

Lesson 6

calendar time; weeks, months and years; Burmese calendar and holidays; voicing; unwritten tones; talking on the telephone; buying a bus ticket

thin-gan:-za chau'   သင်ခန်းစာ ၆   Lesson 6
wɔ:-ha-ṛa   ဝေါဟာရ   Vocabulary

Nouns

ə-pa'	အပတ်	week
pi:-gḛ-dḛ-tə-pa'	ပြီးခဲ့တဲ့တစ်ပတ်	last week, one week ago
nau'-tə-pa'	နောက်တစ်ပတ်	next week, in a week
nau'-thon:-ba'	နောက်သုံးပတ်	in three weeks
lạ	လ	month
pi:-gḛ-dḛ-lạ	ပြီးခဲ့တဲ့လ	last month
pi:-gḛ-dḛ-hnə-lạ	ပြီးခဲ့တဲ့နှစ်လ	two months ago
nau'-lạ	နောက်လ	next month
nau'-thon:-lạ	နောက်သုံးလ	three months from now
be-lạ-le:?	ဘယ်လလဲ	which month?
nau'-ei-pi	နောက်ဧပြီ	next April
hni'	နှစ်	year
pi:-gḛ-dḛ-hni'	ပြီးခဲ့တဲ့နှစ်	last year
nau'-hni'	နောက်နှစ်	next year
ə-the'	အသက်	age
htain-gon	ထိုင်ခုံ	seat
hkə-yi:	ခရီး	trip
hkə-nạ	ခဏ	a moment
nau'-hson:	နောက်ဆုံး	the last one
lạ-zan:	လဆန်း	beginning of the month
lạ-gon	လကုန်	end of the month
lạ-byḛ	လပြည့်	full moon

| la-bye-nei | လပြည့်နေ့ | full moon day |
| la-bye-nya | လပြည့်ည | full moon night |

Verbs

le-de	လည်တယ်	to visit
htwe'-te	ထွက်တယ်	to go out, leave
hkə-yi:-thwa:-de	ခရီးသွားတယ်	to travel
ja-de	ကြာတယ်	to take, last, elapse
be...ja-le:?	ဘယ်...ကြာလဲ။	How long?/How many (hrs., days, etc.)?
win-de	ဝင်တယ်	to enter
thwa:-ei'-te	သွားအိပ်တယ်	to go to bed
ei'-pyɔ-de	သွားအိပ်တယ်	to go to sleep
ei'-ya-hta-de	အိပ်ရာထတယ်	to wake up, get up
ə-na:-yu-de	အနားယူတယ်	to rest
saun-de	စောင့်တယ်	to wait

Particles

pi:-ge-de-	ပြီးခဲ့တဲ့	last, ago
nau'-	နောက်	next
ə-hti	အထိ	until
-ka...-hti	က....ထိ	from...until
thon:-na-yi-ga lei:-na-yi-hti		from 3 to 4 o'clock
သုံးနာရီက လေးနာရီထိ		
-hpo/bo	ဖို့	in order to
-hsi	ဆီ	noun particle showing direction of action to or from a person

		(no English equiv.)
-pe:/be:	ပဲ	only, just
		(suffix used for emphasis)
da-be:-la:?	ဒါပဲလား။	is that all?
-saun	စောင်	counter for documents, letters, tickets...

Other Words and Phrases

ə-mye:-dan:	အမြဲတမ်း	always
tə'-hka-tə-lei	တစ်ခါတလေ	sometimes
pon-hman	ပုံမှန်	usually
da-bei-me̞	ဒါပေမဲ့	but
nau'-hma̞ twei-me	နောက်မှ တွေ့မယ်	"See you later."
hkə-na̞ saun-ba.	ခဏစောင့်ပါ။	"One moment, please."

Days of the Week

tə-nin:-gə-nwei-nei̞	တနင်္ဂနွေနေ့	Sunday
tə-nin:-la-nei̞	တနလ်္ာနေ့	Monday
in-ga-nei̞	အင်္ဂါနေ့	Tuesday
bo'-də-hu:-nei̞	ဗုဒ္ဓဟူးနေ့	Wednesday
ja-dhə-bə-dei:-nei̞	ကြာသပတေးနေ့	Thursday
thau'-ja-nei̞	သောကြာနေ့	Friday
sə-nei-nei̞	စနေနေ့	Saturday

thə-da   သဒ္ဒါ   Grammar

The Burmese Calendar, Climate and Holidays

Myanmar uses both the Western and (Buddhist) lunar calendars.
Lunar months are just 29-1/2 days long, so a second Wazo is
added about every three years to keep the calendars aligned.
Consequently, traditional Burmese holidays do not have an exact
Western calendar date. The two calendars roughly correspond as
follows:

Month	Burmese Name	Corresponding Burmese Month
January	zan-nə-wa-ri ဇန်နဝါရီ	pya-tho ပြာသို
February	hpei-bɔ-wa-ri ဖေဖော်ဝါရီ	də-bọ-dwe: တပို့တွဲ
March	ma' မတ်	də-baun: တပေါင်း
April	ei-pi ဧပြီ	də-gu: တန်ခူး
May	mei မေ	kə-hson ကဆုန်
June	zun ဇွန်	nə-yon နယုန်
July	zu-lain ဇူလိုင်	wa-zo ဝါဆို
August	ɔ-go' သြဂုတ်	wa-gaun ဝါခေါင်
September	se'-tin-ba စက်တင်ဘာ	tɔ-dhə-lin: တော်သလင်း
October	au'-to-ba အောက်တိုဘာ	thə-din:-jju' သီတင်းကျွတ်
November	no-win-ba နိုဝင်ဘာ	də-zaun-mon: တန်ဆောင်မုန်း
December	di-zin-ba ဒီဇင်ဘာ	nə-dɔ နတ်တော်

Myanmar has three seasons: cold, hot and rainy. In October, northerly winds bring cool, dry air. This changes to southerly winds in February, which bring hot, dry air for about three months. Late in the hot season, rains become frequent. By June, frequent, heavy showers mark the rainy season's start. The names of these seasons are:

Hot season   nwei-ya-dhi   နွေရာသီ
Rainy season   mo:-ya-dhi   မိုးရာသီ
Cold season   hsaun:-ya-dhi   ဆောင်းရာသီ

The main holidays in Myanmar are Thingyan or the Water Festival in April, and Thadingyut or the Festival of Lights, marking the end of Buddhist Lent in October. Besides the main holidays, there are also numerous local festivals (called a "pwe:" in Burmese) held at pagodas around the country and include both Buddhist and spirit or "nat" festivals. Nearly all festivals are held on the night of the full moon.

Noun Particle: -hsi -ဆီ (shows movement to or from a person)

When a person is the direct object of a sentence, the -hsi ဆီ
particle must be used to instead of ko or ka. For example:

I will visit Kyaw.

kyaw-hsi thwa:-le-me.   ကျော်ဆီ သွားလည်မယ်။

General Particle: -pe:/be: ဲ (emphasis)

The final sentence particle -pe:/be: ဲ is used to emphasize the
subject of the sentence. English speakers often do this using
inflection, or through words like "just", "really" and "only".

Just bring water, please.   yei pe: pei:-ba   ရေ ဲ ပေး ပါ။

Just looking, (please).   ji-da-ba-be: ကြည့်တာပါဲ။

This curry is really good.   di hin:-be: kaun:-de.

ဒီဟင်းဲ ကောင်းတယ်။

Conversation 1

Zaw   he:-lo.
ဇော်   ဟဲလို။
           Hello?

Ron   he:-lo, mạ-nan-da shị-la:?
ရန်   ဟဲလို၊ မနန္ဒာ ရှိလား။
           Hello, is Ma Nanda there?

Zaw   ho'-kẹ, shị-ba-de.
ဇော်   ဟုတ်ကဲ့၊ ရှိပါတယ်။
           Yes, she's here.

Ron   pyɔ:-lọ yạ-mə-la:?.
ရန်   ပြောလို့ ရမလား။
           May I speak [with her]?

Zaw   yạ-de, hkə-nạ saun-ba.
ဇော်   ရတယ်၊ ခဏ စောင့်ပါ။
           All right, please wait a moment.

Nanda   he:-lo.
နန္ဒာ   ဟဲလို။
           Hello?

Ron   he:-lo, jə-nɔ ron-ba. ba lo'-nei-le:?
ရန်   ဟဲလို၊ ကျွန်တော် ရန်ပါ။ ဘာ လုပ်နေလဲ။
           Hi, this is Ron. What are you doing?

Nanda   ba-hma̱ mə-lo'-hpu:.
နန္ဒာ   ဘာမှ မလုပ်ဘူး။
           I'm not doing anything.

Ron   di-nya̱ mei'-hswei-nẹ htə-min: thwa:-sa:-me.
           lai'-mə-la:?
ရာန်   ဒီည မိတ်ဆွေနဲ့ ထမင်း သွားစားမယ်။
           လိုက်မလား။
           Tonight, a friend and I are going out to eat.
           Do you want to come along?
           (lit., "Will you follow?")

Nanda   lai'-me. be-ə-chein thwa:-mə-le:?
နန္ဒာ   လိုက်မယ်။ ဘယ်အချိန် သွားမလဲ။
           [I] will come. What time are you going?

Ron   jə-nɔ̱ ein-go chau'-na-yi la-gẹ-ba.
ရာန်   ကျွန်တော့် အိမ်ကို ခြောက်နာရီ လာခဲ့ပါ။
           Please come to my house at 6:00.

Nanda   ya̱-ba-dẹ. chau'-na-yi-hma tweị-me.
နန္ဒာ   ရပါတယ်။ ခြောက်နာရီမှာ တွေ့မယ်။
           I'll do that. See you at 6:00.

Ron   kaun:-bi. da-be:-nɔ̱?
ရာန်   ကောင်းပြီ။ ဒါပဲနော်။
           Great. Goodbye (that's all, isn't it?).

Nanda   da-ba-be:.
နန္ဒာ   ဒါပါပဲ။
           Goodbye (lit.: "that's all").

Conversation 2

Ticket Seller:[27] လက်မှတ် ရောင်းသူ	be-thwa:-mə-le:? ဘယ်သွားမလဲ။ Where are you going?
Customer: ဝယ်သူ	bə-gan-go thwa:-jin-de. bə-gan-go be-hnə-na-yi ja-le:? ပုဂံကို သွားချင်တယ်။ ပုဂံကို ဘယ်နှစ်နာရီ ကြာလဲ။ I want to go to Bagan. How many hours is it to Bagan?
Seller: ရောင်းသူ	ba'-sə-ka:-nẹ hsẹ-hnə-na-yi ja-de. ဘတ်စကားနဲ့ ဆယ့်နှစ်နာရီ ကြာတယ်။ Twelve hours [long] by bus.
Customer: ဝယ်သူ	bə-gan-ka: mə-ne'-hpyan be-hnə-na-yi htwe'-mə-le:? ပုဂံကား မနက်ဖြန် ဘယ်နှစ်နာရီ ထွက်မလဲ။ What time will buses go to Bagan tomorrow?
Seller: ရောင်းသူ	nyạ-nei thon:-na-yi, nga:-na-yi, hkun-nə-na-yi. ညနေ သုံးနာရီ ၊ ငါးနာရီ ၊ ခုနှစ်နာရီ။ Three [in the afternoon], five and seven.

---

[27] Ticket Seller: Le'-ma' yaun:-dhu, Customer: we-dhu.

Customer:	nyạ-nei nga:-na-yi thwa:-ɉin-de.
ဝယ်သူ	ə-sheị-hma htain-gon shị-dhei:-la:?
	ညနေ ငါးနာရီ သွားချင်တယ်။
	အရှေ့မှာ ထိုင်ခုံ ရှိသေးလား။
	I want to leave at 5 p.m.
	Do you still have any seats in front?

Seller:	shị-ba-de. be-hnə-saun lo-ɉin-ba-le:.
ရောင်းသူ	ရှိပါတယ်။ ဘယ်နှစ်စောင် လိုချင်ပါလဲ။
	[We] do. How many tickets do you want?

Customer:	tə-saun yu-me.
ဝယ်သူ	တစ်စောင် ယူမယ်။
	I'll take one ticket.

Seller:	nga:-daun.
ရောင်းသူ	ငါးထောင်။
	Five thousand.

Customer:	di-hma. jei:-zu:-be:.
ဝယ်သူ	ဒီမှာ။ ကျေးဇူးပဲ။
	Here [is the money]. Thanks.

wa-ja̱-mya: ဝါကျများ Sentences

1. A: di-nya̱, ba lo'-chin-le:?
ဒီည ဘာ လုပ်ချင်လဲ။
What do you want to do tonight?

B: di-nya̱ ə-pyin-hma thwa:-sa:-ɟin-de.
ဒီည အပြင်မှာ သွားစားချင်တယ်။
I want to go out to eat tonight.

2. A: mə-nei̱-ga̱ be thwa:-le:?
မနေ့က ဘယ် သွားလဲ။
Where did you go yesterday?

B: mə-nei̱-ga̱ shwe-də-gon hpə-ya: thwa:-de.
မနေ့က ရွှေတိဂုံ ဘုရား သွားတယ်။
Yesterday, I went to Shwedagon Pagoda.

3. A: mə-ne'-hpyan be-thwa:-le-ɟin-le:?
မနက်ဖြန် ဘယ်သွားလည် ချင်လဲ။
Where would you like to visit tomorrow?

B: mə-ne'-hpyan mei'-hswei-hsi thwa:-le-me.
မနက်ဖြန် မိတ်ဆွေဆီ သွားလည်မယ်။
Tomorrow, I will go visit friends.

4. A: ein be-don:-ga̱ we-le:?
အိမ် ဘယ်တုန်းက ဝယ်လဲ။
When did you buy a house?

B: pi:-ge̱-de̱ thon:-la̱-ga̱ ein we-de.
ပြီးခဲ့တဲ့ သုံးလက အိမ် ဝယ်တယ်။
I bought a house three months ago.

5.   A: se'-bein: be-dɔ̰ we-mə-le:?
            စက်ဘီး ဘယ်တော့ ဝယ်မလဲ။
            When do you want to buy a bicycle?

      B: nau'-lạ-hma se'-bein: we-me.
            နောက်လမှာ စက်ဘီး ဝယ်မယ်။
            I will buy a bicycle next month.

      C: no-win-ba-lạ-hma se'-bein: we-me.
            နိုဝင်ဘာလမှာ စက်ဘီး ဝယ်မယ်။
            I will buy a bicycle this coming November.

6.   A: be-neị na:-jin-le:?
            ဘယ်နေ့ နားချင်လဲ။
            What day [do you] want off?

      B: sə-nei-neị-hma na:-jin-de.
            စနေနေ့မှာ နားချင်တယ်။
            [I] want Saturday off.

7.   A: be-neị-dwei ə-lo'-lo'-thə-le:?
            ဘယ်နေ့တွေ အလုပ်လုပ်သလဲ။
            What days do you work?

      B: ja-dhə-bə-dei:-neị-nẹ sə-nei-neị-hma ə-lo'-lo'-te.
            ကြာသပတေးနေ့နဲ့ စနေနေ့မှာ အလုပ်လုပ်တယ်။
            I work on Thursday and Saturday.

8.   jaun:-hma shi'-na-yi-gạ hsẹ-hnə-na-yi-hti shị-de.
            ကျောင်းမှာ ရှစ်နာရီက ဆယ့်နှစ်နာရီထိ ရှိတယ်။
            I was at school from 8:00 until 12:00.

9.   A: pon-hman be-ə-chein ei'-le:?
          ပုံမှန် ဘယ်အချိန် အိပ်လဲ။
          When do you usually go to sleep?

     B: pon-hman ei'-ya-go hsẹ-tə-na-yi-hma win-de.
          ပုံမှန် အိပ်ရာကို ဆယ့်တစ်နာရီမှာ ဝင်တယ်။
          I usually go to bed at 11:00.

10. A: nin ba lo'-da jai'-le:?
          နင် ဘာ လုပ်တာ ကြိုက်လဲ။
          What do you like to do?

     B: ti-bi jị-da jai'-te.
          တီဗီ ကြည့်တာ ကြိုက်တယ်။
          I like to watch television.

11.   hpei-bɔ-wa-ri-lạ-gạ ei-pi-lạ-hti jə-pan-hma nei-de.
          ဖေဖော်ဝါရီလက ဧပြီလထိ ဂျပန်မှာ နေတယ်။
          I live in Japan from February to April.

12.   se'-tin-ba-lạ-hma hpə-ya:-bwe: jị-bọ in:-lei:-kan-go
          thwa:-jin-de.
          စက်တင်ဘာလမှာ ဘုရားပွဲ ကြည့်ဖို့ အင်းလေးကန်ကို
          သွားချင်တယ်။
          In September, I want to go to Inle Lake to see the
          Pagoda Festival.

13.   mə-ne'-hpyan bi-za yạ-bọ htain:-than-yon: thwa:-me.
          မနက်ဖြန် ဗီဇာ ရဖို့ ထိုင်းသံရုံး သွားမယ်။
          Tomorrow, I will go to the Thai embassy in order to
          get a visa.

14. A: ə-the' be-lau'-le:?
အသက် ဘယ်လောက်လဲ။
How old are you?

B: ə-the' hnə'-hsẹ-nga:-hni' shị-bị.
အသက် နှစ်ဆယ့်ငါးနှစ် ရှိပြီ။
I am twenty-five years old.

15. A: man-də-lei:-hma be-lau' ja-mə-le:?
မန္တလေးမှာ ဘယ်လောက် ကြာမလဲ။
How long will you be in Mandalay?

B: hnə-ba' ja-me.
နှစ်ပတ် ကြာမယ်။
[I'll] be there for two weeks.

16. A: myan-ma-nain-gan yau'-ta ja-bị-la:?
မြန်မာနိုင်ငံ ရောက်တာ ကြာပြီလား။
Have you been in Myanmar long?

B: tə-lạ ja-bị.
တစ်လ ကြာပြီ။
For one month.

17. tə-nya-lon: ei'-mə-pyɔ-bu:.
တစ်ညလုံး အိပ်မပျော်ဘူး
I didn't sleep all night.

Drills

1. Practice saying the following sentences in Myanmar. Some sentences can be said in different ways. If the sentence is a question, practice answering it too.

Yesterday, I went to the movie theater.

_____

I go to Myanmar in order to study the Myanmar language.

_____

I usually read the newspaper in the morning.

_____

When did you go to Bagan?

_____

What months were you in France?

_____

2. Do the following.

Create a two person dialogue about a trip you are planning. Include when you are leaving and the length of time that you will be gone in months.

Compose a paragraph telling when you usually go to sleep, how long you sleep and when you usually wake up.

3. Use the following words to form ten sentences.

shin ရှင်   -po̞/bo̞ ဖို့   win-de ဝင်တယ်
ə-the' အသက်   thin-de သင်တယ်   ə-lo'-lo'-de
                                            အလုပ်လုပ်တယ်
jaun: ကျောင်း   ei-pi ဧပြီ   tə-nei̞-ga̞ တနေ့က
jə-ma̞ ကျွန်မ   se'-tin-ba စက်တင်ဘာ   gə-za:-de ကစားတယ်
thu သူ   twei̞-de တွေ့တယ်   bu-da-yon ဘူတာရုံ
thwa:-le သွားလည်   shi̞-de ရှိတယ်   lo'-chin-de
                                            လုပ်ချင်တယ်
nga: ငါး   we-de ဝယ်တယ်   tə-nin:-la-nei̞
                                            တနင်္လာနေ့
ə-pɔ အပေါ်   lo'-de လုပ်တယ်   mə-ne'-hpyan
                                            မနက်ဖြန်
sa-o' စာအုပ်   pa' ပတ်   a:-la'-ye'
                                            အားလပ်ရက်
-hma မှာ   la̞ လ   ta'-hka-tə-lei
                                            တစ်ခါတလေ
ka: ကား   -hti̞ ထိ   pi:-ge̞-de̞-la̞ ပြီးခဲ့တဲ့လ

Test 6

Match the following days and months with the appropriate Burmese word.

Months

_____ 1. January   a. မေ

_____ 2. February   b. ဒီဇင်ဘာ

_____ 3. March   c. သြဂုတ်

_____ 4. April   d. စက်တင်ဘာ

_____ 5. May   e. ဇူလိုင်

_____ 6. June   f. နိုဝင်ဘာ

_____ 7. July   g. အောက်တိုဘာ

_____ 8. August   h. မတ်

_____ 9. September   i. ဇန်နဝါရီ

_____ 10. October   j. ဇွန်

_____ 11. November   k. ဧပြီ

_____ 12. December   l. ဖေဖော်ဝါရီ

Days

_____ 1. Monday   a. ja-dhə-bə-dei-neị ကြာသပတေးနေ့

_____ 2. Tuesday   b. bo'-də-hu:-neị ဗုဒ္ဓဟူးနေ့

_____ 3. Wednesday   c. tə-nin:-la-neị တနင်္လာနေ့

_____ 4. Thursday   d. sə-nei-neị စနေနေ့

_____ 5. Friday   e. thau'-ja-neị သောကြာနေ့

_____ 6. Saturday   f. tə-nin:-gə-nwei-neị တနင်္ဂနွေနေ့

_____ 7. Sunday   g. in-ga-neị အင်္ဂါနေ့

Translate the following into English or Myanmar.

1. စနေနေ့က တနင်္လာနေ့ထိ နားတယ်။

_____

2. တစ်ခါတလေ သန်းခေါင်မှာ အိပ်တယ်။

_____

3. နောက်အပတ်မှာ ဗီယက်နမ် သွားမယ်။

_____

4. Two months from now, I will go to Mandalay.

_____

5. He has been waiting since six o'clock.

_____

Reading & Writing

Voicing and The Voicing Rule

Both English and Burmese have both unvoiced and voiced consonants. Voicing means making a humming sound in the voicebox while saying a consonant. For example, the consonant "b" is voiced, while "p" sound is not. In Burmese, there are a number of "voiceable" consonants, that is, consonants that shift from unvoiced to a voiced pronunciation. The folllowing chart lists both the unvoiced and corresponding voiced consonants:

Unvoiced Consonants:

/k/ /hk/ /j/ /ch/ /s/ /hs/ /t/ /ht/ /p/ /hp/ /th/

က   ခ   ကျ   ချ   စ   ဆ   တ   ထ   ပ   ဖ   သ

gets voiced to:

/g/   /j/   /z/   /d/   /b/   /dh/

These unvoiced consonants get voiced according to the following rule: the second and following syllables are voiced, unless they follow a syllable that ends with a glottal stop. For example, the verb particle -te တယ် is usually voiced to -de:

[he/she] eats	စားတယ်	(sa:-de)	or
[he/she] goes	သွားတယ်	(thwa:-de)	

but note that

[he/she] likes	ကြိုက်တယ်	(jai'-te)

is *not* voiced because of the glottal stop.

The voicing rule applies to particles added to the end of a word, but not to the first syllable of the following word, so care must be taken to understand where words end in order to voice the consonants correctly. Consonants are also not voiced in syllables following the အ prefix.

Other Voicing Examples:

ချင် (chin, want) > စားချင် (sa:-**jin**, want to eat)

ရည်းစား (yi:-**za:**, boyfriend/girlfriend)

ဆိုင် (hsain, shop) > ထမင်းဆိုင်(htə-min:-**zain**, restaurant)

သတင်းစာ (thə-**din:-za**, newspaper)

အိမ်ထောင် (ein-**daun**, marriage)

လယ်သမား (le-**dhə**-ma:, farmer)

Exceptions to the Voicing Rule

There are many exceptions to the voicing rule. Initial consonants in some words are voiced (these are discussed in Lesson 9), while other consonants are not voiced, even though they look like they should be. A seeming exception is that a syllable following one with a weakened vowel that includes a glottal stop is still pronounced as if the glottal stop were pronounced. It is therefore not voiced even though it sounds like it should be. For example: is in

the word for ten: တစ်ဆယ် is pronounced   tə-hse (*not* tə-ze).

"Hidden" compound words make up another group of exceptions. In such cases, the word is pronounced as if its components are separate words. For instance, the verb for listen (literally "to stand in the ear"), begins with "ear" (နား) is not voiced:

na:-htaun *not* na:-daun နားထောင် (listen)

Writing Exercise 6

Translate and transliterate the following sentences into Burmese. Mark *all* voiced consonants and make sure to be aware of exceptions to the voicing rule in these examples.

1. Five thousand forty, please.

2. [I] want to go to the university in the afternoon.

3. No. [He] doesn't come from Bago.

4. Thank you. Goodbye ("[I] have gone.")

5. [The] Burmese language is not difficult.

6. Can you write in Myanmar?

7. [I] have already been to Shwedagon Pagoda.

8. [He] went to Yangon six months ago.

9. Nice to meet [you].

10. [I] want to read a book.

Lesson 7

foods; forms of address; informal pronouns; talking
to monks; have ever; eating in a restaurant; eating at
a teashop; weakening

thin-gan:-za hkhu-ni' သင်ခန်းစာ ၇   Lesson 7
wɔ:-ha-ra̩   ဝေါဟာရ   Vocabulary

Nouns

ba-hpyi'-lo̩...le:	ဘာဖြစ်လို့...လဲ	Why?
ba-hpyi'-lo̩ la-le:	ဘာဖြစ်လို့ လာလဲ။	"Why have you come?"
ba-jaun̩	ဘာကြောင့်	because
min, nin	မင်း၊ နင်	you (informal)
nga	ငါ	I (informal)
thei' mə...bu:	သိပ် မ...ဘူး	not so...
myan-ma-ə-sa:-ə-sa	မြန်မာအစားအစာ	Myanmar cuisine/food
htain:-ə-sa:-ə-sa	ထိုင်းအစားအစာ	Thai food
tə-yo'-ə-sa:-ə-sa	တရုတ်အစားအစာ	Chinese food
ə-sa'	အစပ်	spicy food
ə-cho-bwe:	အချိုပွဲ	dessert
mi:-bo-jaun	မီးဖိုချောင်	kitchen
ne:-ne:-hta'	နည်းနည်းထပ်	a little bit more
da:	ဓား	knife
zun:	ဇွန်း	spoon
hkə-yin:	ခက်ရင်း	fork
tu	တူ	chopsticks
`hin:-ɟo	ဟင်းချို	soup
htə-min:-ɟɔ	ထမင်းကြော်	fried rice
yei-than̩	ရေသန့်	purified (bottled) water
ə-ye	အရည်	juice

kei'-moṇ	ကိတ်မုန့်	cake
paun-moṇ	ပေါင်မုန့်	bread
-hkwe'/gwe'	ခွက်	up (also a counter word)
nau'-tə-hkwe'	နောက်တစ်ခွက်	another cup
-pwe:/bwe:	ပွဲ	serving or bowl (also a counter word)
-lon:	လုံး	bottle (counter word)
nau'-tə-lon:	နောက်တစ်လုံး	another bottle

Verbs

bai'-hsa-de	ဗိုက်ဆာတယ်	to be hungry
mei:-de	မေးတယ်	to ask something
taun:-de	တောင်းတယ်	to ask for something
shin:-me	ရှင်းမယ်	to clear [the bill]
jɔ-de	ကြော်တယ်	to fry
thaṇ-de	သန့်တယ်	to be clean, pure
thon:-de	သုံးတယ်	to use
che'-pyo'-te	ချက်ပြုတ်တယ်	to cook
hli:-de	လှီးတယ်	to cut, peel, slice
mya:-thwa:-de	များသွားတယ်	to be too much
cho-de	ချိုတယ်	to be sweet[28]
chin-de	ချဉ်တယ်	to be sour

---

[28] Cho-de is often used to refer to dishes that are not spicy (w/o chili) as well.

ngan-de	ငန်တယ်	to be salty
hka:-de	ခါးတယ်	to be bitter
sa'-te	စပ်တယ်	to be spicy (hot)
mə-sa'-hpu:	မစပ်ဘူး။	"It's not spicy."
pɔ-de	ပေါ့တယ်	to be bland, tasteless
wạ-de	ဝတယ်	to be fat, satisfied
wạ-bi	ဝပြီ။	"I'm full."
ə-yə-dha	အရသာ	delicious, tasty (adv)
ə-yə-dha shị-de	အရသာ ရှိတယ်။	"It's delicious."
ə-yə-dha mə-shị-bu:	အရသာ မရှိဘူး။	"It's not tasty."

Particles

-lọ	လို့	because
-on:	ဦး	indicates further action
-hpu:/bu:	ဖူး	have ever done something

More Food Nouns

ə-tha:	အသား	**Meat**
ə-me:-dha:	အမဲသား	beef
je'-tha:	ကြက်သား	chicken
we'-tha:	ဝက်သား	pork
nga:	ငါး	fish

ə-thi:	အသီး	**Fruit**
pan:-dhi:	ပန်းသီး	apple
htɔ-ba'-thi:	ထောပတ်သီး	avocado
nge'-pyɔ:-dhi:	ငှက်ပျောသီး	banana
on:-dhi:	အုန်းသီး	coconut
ɔ:-za-dhi:	သြဇာသီး	custard apple
du:-yen:-dhi:	ဒူးရင်းသီး	durian
zə-byi'-thi:	စပျစ်သီး	grapes
ma-lə-ka-dhi:	မာလကာသီး	guava
pein:-ne:-dhi:	ပိန္နဲသီး	jackfruit
than-bə-ya-dhi:	သံပုရာသီး	lime
lain-chi:-dhi:	လိုင်ချီးသီး	lychee
thə-ye'-thi:	သရက်သီး	mango
min:-gu'-thi:	မင်းကွတ်သီး	mangosteen
lein-mɔ-dhi:	လိမ္မော်သီး	orange
thin:-bɔ:-dhi:	သင်္ဘောသီး	papaya
thi'-tɔ-dhi:	သစ်တော်သီး	pear
na-na'-thi:	နာနတ်သီး	pineapple
zi:-dhi:	ဆီးသီး	plum
jwe:-gɔ:-dhi:	ကျွဲကောသီး	pomelo
je'-mau'-thi:	ကြက်မောက်သီး	rambutan
hpə-ye:-dhi:	ဖရဲသီး	watermelon

hin:-dhi:-hin:-ywe' ဟင်းသီးဟင်းရွက်   Vegetables

gaw-bi-do'	ဂေါ်ဖီထုပ်	cabbage
mon-la-ṵ-ni	မုန်လာဥနီ	carrots
pyaun:-bu:	ပြောင်းဖူး	corn
je'-thun-byu	ကြက်သွန်ဖြူ	garlic
jin:	ဂျင်း	ginger
hsə-la'-ywe'	ဆလတ်ရွက်	lettuce
hmo	မှို	mushrooms
je'-thun-ni	ကြက်သွန်နီ	onions
shwei-be:	ရွှေပဲသီး	snow peas
myei-be:	မြေပဲ	peanuts
hin:-nu-nwe	ဟင်းနုနွယ်	amaranth
pe:-dauṇ-she	ပဲတောင့်ရှည်	string beans
hkə-yan:-dhi:	ခရမ်းသီး	eggplant, aubergine
hkə-yan:-jin-dhi:	ခရမ်းချဉ်သီး	tomato

Tea Shop Beverages

le'-hpe'-yei	လက်ဖက်ရည်	black tea (w/ milk+sugar)
yei-nwe:, yei-nwe:-jan:	ရေနွေး၊ ရေနွေးကြမ်း	plain (olong) tea
kɔ-hpi	ကော်ဖီ	coffee (w/ milk+sugar)
nwa:-nṵ	နွားနို့	cow's milk
nṵ-nɛ̰	နို့နဲ့	with milk
kɔ-hpi-nṵ-nɛ̰	ကော်ဖီနို့နဲ့	coffee with milk

lein-mɔ-ye	လိမ္မော်ရည်	orange juice
hso-da	ဆိုဒါ	soda water
yei-ge:	ရေခဲ	ice
kɔ-hpi-ei:	ကော်ဖီအေး	iced coffee
thə-ja:	သကြား	sugar
jan-ye	ကြံရည်	sugar cane juice
bi-ya	ဘီယာ	beer

Some Typical Burmese Foods

pə-la-ta	ပလာတာ	parata
sə-mu-hsa	စမူဆာ	samosa
pau'-si	ပေါက်စီ	Chinese steamed dumpling
hkau'-hswe:	ခေါက်ဆွဲ	noodles
hkau'-hswe:-jɔ	ခေါက်ဆွဲကြော်	fried noodles
moṇ-hin:-ga:	မုန့်ဟင်းခါး	mohinga
shan:-hkau'-hswe:	ရှမ်းခေါက်ဆွဲ	Shan noodles
hin:	ဟင်း	curry
bə-zun-hin:	ပုဇွန်ဟင်း	shrimp curry
nga:-baun:	ငါးပေါင်း	steamed fish
le'-hpe'-tho'	လက်ဖက်သုပ်	pickled tea salad
jin-dho'	ဂျင်းသုပ်	ginger salad
kau'-hnyin:	ကောက်ညှင်း	sticky rice

thə-da   သဒ္ဒါ   Grammar

Level of Formality

In this lesson, we'll review pronouns, and the use of kinship terms and other forms of address used in everyday life. Three factors determine what term one should use in conversation with another person: familiarity, age difference and social status.

Pronouns: Formal and Informal forms of "You and I"

- The pronouns min: (မင်း) and nin (နင်) are commonly used for "you" but only between close friends and siblings, so a beginning Burmese student may not hear these words in direct conversation.
- hkə-mya:/shin (ခင်ဗျား၊ ရှင်), are said by the speaker, males use "hkə-mya:", females use "shin". Both are polite terms for "you" used with unfamiliar individuals.
- Likewise, nga (ငါ) is used for "I" between close friends and family of roughly the same age while jə-nɔ and jə-ma̱ are used in less intimate circumstances and with elders.

Forms of Address: Use of Kinship Terms

- A more distant form of "you", using kinship terms, is often used in interacting with waiters, waitresses, taxi drivers, sellers of goods, etc.
- When speaking to a much older person use u:-lei: (ဦးလေး) or dɔ:(ဒေါ်) meaning uncle or aunt, respectively, for "you".
- When speaking to a somewhat older person use ə-ko (အကို) and ə-ma̱ (အမ) meaning elder brother or elder sister, respectively, for "you".
- A man speaking to a somewhat younger person uses nyi-lei: (ညီလေး) and nyi-ma̱-lei: (ညီမလေး) meaning younger brother/sister, respectively.
- A woman uses maun-lei: (မောင်လေး) and nyi-ma̱-lei: (ညီမလေး) to younger man or woman, respectively.

Forms of Address: Equivalents to Mr. and Miss/Mrs.

- In addressing someone as "Mr." use u: (ဦး) for a man that is older than the speaker and maun (မောင်) for one who is younger. In both cases the u: or maun should be followed by the person's name (e.g., maun sein).
- There's no equivalent to Mrs. in Burmese, but there is a distinction between older or younger listeners. An older woman is addressed as dɔ (ဒေါ်) while a younger woman should be called mạ (မ), followed by the person's name.

Forms of Address: Use of hsə-ya ("teacher")

- Teachers should be addressed using hsə-ya (ဆရာ) for a man and hsə-ya-mạ (ဆရာမ) for a woman. This term not only applies to teachers, but also engineers, doctors, managers and some civil servants.

Forms of Address: Talking with Monks

Special forms of address are also used in Burmese to speak to monks. There are three ways to address monks as follows:

- ko-yin ကိုရင် (for a novice, age 6-19)
- u:-zin: ဦးဇင်း (most other monks)
- hpon:-ji: ဘုန်းကြီး (for a monastery's senior monk) .
- A monk calls a lay person də-ga/də-ga-mạ (ဒကာ၊ ဒကာမ)
- Refer to oneself as: tə-bę-dɔ/tə-bę-dɔ-mạ (တပည့်တော်၊ တပည့်တော်မ, meaning student or follower)
- Buddhist nuns (of any age) should be called hsə-ya-lei: (ဆရာလေး)

Verb: -hpu:/bu: ဖူး (have ever)

To say that one has "ever done" something, -hpu:/-bu: (ဖူး) is used:

Have you ever visited Mandalay?　man:-də-lei: thwa:-bu:-dhə-la:.

မန္တလေး သွားဖူးသလား။

Yes, I've visited Mandalay.　ho'-kẹ, man:-də-lei: thwa:-bu:-de.

ဟုတ်ကဲ့ မန္တလေး သွားဖူးတယ်။

No, I have never been to Mandalay.　hin in:, man:-də-lei: mə-
thwa:-bu:-bu:.

ဟင့်အင်း၊ မန္တလေး မသွားဖူးဘူး။

Have you ever eaten mohinga?　moṇ-hin:-ga: sa:-bu:-dhə-la:?

မုန့်ဟင်းခါး စားဖူးသလား။

Yes, I've eaten mohinga before.　in:, moṇ-hin:-ga: sa:-bu:-de.

အင်း၊ မုန့်ဟင်းခါး စားဖူးတယ်။

Clause-ending particles: -lọ လို့ (because), -hpọ/bọ ဖို့ (in order to), -yin ရင် (if)

In Burmese sentence clauses are formed using a clause-ending particle. This is similar to English, except that in Burmese, the "subordinate clause" comes first, not last as in English. The clause-ending particles used in this book are -lo. (because), -hpo./bo. (in order to), and -yin (if).

Here's an example sentence using the lọ particle to mean because:

[I] went to sleep because [I] was tired.　mɔ:-lọ thwa:-ei-de.

မောလို့ သွားအိပ်တယ်။

The -hpo/bo particle has a similar use of providing a kind of explanation for why something needs to be done or why something was done. It can be translated as "for", "to" or "in order to". For example:

He went to the market to buy fruit. ə-thi we-hpọ thu zei:-go thwa:-de.

အသီး ဝယ်ဖို့ သူ ဈေးကို သွားတယ်။

The yin ရင် particle means "if" or "when", in reference to some future action. Such sentences in English would have one clause starting with if and another starting with then, but Burmese only uses the -yin ရင် particle at the end of the subordinate clause.

If I have time, I will go there. ə-chein shị-yin, thwa:-me.

အချိန် ရှိရင် သွားမယ်။

Verb Particle: -on: ဦး (further action)

The -on: ဦး verb particle indicates an action will be carried on further. A very common phrase which uses this particle is said when negotiating a price with a vendor:

That's expensive. Can you lower [the price] more? zei:-mya:-de. shọ-ba-on:-la:? ဈေးများတယ်။ လျှော့ပါဦးလား။

Conversation 1

Customer: nyi-lei:, nyi-lei: ...
ဝယ်သူ ညီလေး ၊ ညီလေး။
Waiter, waiter.

Waiter: ba thau'-mə-le:?
စားပွဲထိုး ဘာ သောက်မလဲ။
What will you drink?

Customer: la'-hpe'-ye tə-hkwe'.
ဝယ်သူ လက်ဖက်ရည် တစ်ခွက်။
A cup of tea, please.

Waiter: ba sa:-mə-le.
စားပွဲထိုး ဘာ စားမလဲ။
What do you want to eat?

Customer: sə-mu-sa-tho' tə-bwe:.
ဝယ်သူ စမူဆာသုပ် တစ်ပွဲ။
A samosa salad.

... Later ....

Customer: ဝယ်သူ	nyi-lei: shin:-me. ညီလေး ရှင်းမယ်။ Waiter, the bill!
Waiter: စားပွဲထိုး	thon:-ya nga:-ze-ba. သုံးရာ ငါးဆယ်ပါ။ Three hundred fifty, please.
Customer: ဝယ်သူ	di-hma. ဒီမှာ။ Here.
Waiter: စားပွဲထိုး	jei:-zu:-be:. ကျေးဇူးပဲ။ Thanks.

Conversation 2

Waiter: htain-ba. ba-sa:-mə-le:?
စားပွဲထိုး ထိုင်ပါ။ ဘာစားမလဲ။
Please sit down. What do you want to eat?

Customer: nga:-hin: tə-bwe:-ye hka-yan:-ɟin-dhi:-tho' tə-bwe:-ye
htə-min: nhə-bwe:.
ဝယ်သူ ငါးဟင်း တစ်ပွဲရယ် ခရမ်းချဉ်သီးသုပ် တစ်ပွဲရယ် ထမင်း နှစ်ပွဲ။
A plate fish curry and a plate of tomato salad and two plates of steamed rice.

Waiter: ba thau'-mə-le:.
စားပွဲထိုး ဘာ သောက်မလဲ။
What would you like to drink?

Customer: than-bə-ya-yei tə-hkwe'-ne̥ la'-hpe'-ye tə-hkwe'.
ဝယ်သူ သံပုရာရည် တစ်ခွက်နဲ့ လက်ဖက်ရည် တစ်ခွက်။
A glass of lime juice and a glass of plain tea.

Waiter: da-be:-la:?
စားပွဲထိုး ဒါပဲလား။
Is that all?

Customer: da-ba-be:.
ဝယ်သူ ဒါပါပဲ။
[Yes], that's it.

... Later ....

Waiter:	di-hma.
စားပွဲထိုး	ဒီမှာ။
	Here you go.

Customer:	di-ha mə-hma-bu:.
ဝယ်သူ	ဒီဟာ မမှာဘူး။
	I didn't order that!

Waiter:	o, hsɔ:-ri:.
စားပွဲထိုး	အို ဆောရီး။
	Oh, sorry.

... Still Later ....

Customer:	nya-ma̯-lei:, shin:-me.
ဝယ်သူ	ညီမလေး ရှင်းမယ်။
	Waiter, the bill!

Waiter:	chau'-ya nga:-ze-ba.
စားပွဲထိုး	ခြောက်ရာ ငါးဆယ်ပါ။
	Six hundred and fifty, please.

Customer:	di-hma.
ဝယ်သူ	ဒီမှာ။
	Here.

Waiter:	jei:-zu:-tin-ba-de.
စားပွဲထိုး	ကျေးဇူးတင်ပါတယ်။
	Thanks.

wa-ja̱-mya: ဝါကျများ   Sentences

1. A: di yo'-shin ji̱-pi:-bi-la:?
         ဒီ ရုပ်ရှင် ကြည့်ပြီးပြီလား။
         Have you seen this movie yet?

    B: di yo'-shin ji̱-pi:-bi.
         ဒီ ရုပ်ရှင် ကြည့်ပြီးပြီ။
         I have already seen this movie.

    C: ta̱-hka-hma ma̱-ji̱-bu:-bu:.
         တခါမှ မကြည့်ဖူးဘူး။
         I have never seen it.

2. A: hsai-ka: si:-bu:-la:?
         ဆိုက်ကား စီးဖူးလား။
         Have you ever ridden in a "sidecar"?

    B: ho'-ke̱, si:-bu:-de.
         ဟုတ်ကဲ့ စီးဖူးတယ်။
         Yes, I have ridden in (one).

3.   ba̱-gan-go yau'-hpu-ba-de.
         ပုဂံကို ရောက်ဖူးပါတယ်။
         I have been to Bagan.

4. A: myan-ma-a̱-sa:-a̱-sa thei' sa'-tha̱-la:?
         မြန်မာအစားအစာ သိပ် စပ်သလား။
         Is Myanmar food very spicy?

    B: myan-ma-a̱-sa:-a̱-sa thei' ma̱-sa'-hpu:.
         မြန်မာအစားအစာ သိပ် မစပ်ဘူး။
         Myanmar food is not very spicy.

5.   A: tə-yo'-ə-sa:-ə-sa ba-hpyi'-lọ mə-jai'-ta-le:?
          တရတ်အစားအစာ ဘာဖြစ်လို့ မကြိုက်တာလဲ။
          Why don't you like Chinese food?

     B: tə-yo'-ə-sa:-ə-sa mə-sa'-lọ.
          တရတ်အစာအစား မစပ်လို့။
          Because Chinese food is not spicy.

6.   A: thụ-hma ka: ba-hpyi'-lọ mə-shị-da-le:?
          သူ့မှာ ကား ဘာဖြစ်လို့ မရှိတာလဲ။
          Why doesn't he have a car?

     B: thụ-hma pai'-hsan mə-shị-lọ ka: mə-we-yạ-bu:.
          သူ့မှာ ပိုက်ဆံ မရှိလို့ ကား မဝယ်ရဘူး။
          Because he doesn't have money, he doesn't have a car.

7.   A: thu ba-hpyi'-lọ che'-pyo'-ta me-jai'-le:?
          သူ ဘာဖြစ်လို့ ချက်ပြုတ်တာ မကြိုက်လဲ။
          Why doesn't she like cooking?

     B: thu che'-pyo'-ta mə-jai'-lọ mə-che'-te'-hpu:.
          သူ ချက်ပြုတ်တာ မကြိုက်လို့ မချက်တတ်ဘူး။
          She doesn't like to cook because she can't cook.

8.   A: di hin-jo kaun:-la:?
          ဒီ ဟင်းချို ကောင်းလား။
          Is this soup good?

     B: ho'-kẹ, di hin-jo ə-yə-dha shị-de.
          ဟုတ်ကဲ့၊ ဒီ ဟင်းချို အရသာ ရှိတယ်။
          Yes, this soup is delicious.

     C: mə-kaun:-hpu:. di hin-jo ə-yə-dha mə-shị-bu:.
          မကောင်းဘူး။ ဒီ ဟင်းချို အရသာ မရှိဘူး။
          No. It's not tasty.

D: mə-kaun:-hpu:. ə-yan: ŋan-lọ sa:-mə-kaun:-bu:..

မကောင်းဘူး။ အရမ်း ငန်လို့ စားမကောင်းဘူး။

No. It doesn't taste good because it's too salty.

9. A: hta'-yu-on:-mə-la:?

ထပ်ယူဦးမလား။

Will you take a bit more?

B: ne:-ne: hta'-yu-on:-me.

နည်းနည်း ထပ်ယူဦးမယ်။

I'll have a bit more.

C: yạ-ba-de. wạ- bi. jei:-zu:-be:.

ရပါတယ်။ ဝပြီ။ ကျေးဇူးပဲ။

That's all right. I'm full. Thanks.

10. A: ə-sa' jai'-thə-la:?

အစပ် ကြိုက်သလား။

Do you like spicy food?

B: jai'-te.

ကြိုက်တယ်။

I like it.

C: mə-jai'-hpu:.

မကြိုက်ဘူး။

I don't like it.

11. hin:-dhi-hin-ywe'-go da:-nẹ hli:-de.

ဟင်းသီးဟင်းရွက်ကို ဓါးနဲ့ လှီးတယ်။

I cut vegetables with a knife.

12. kɔ-hpi-ei: jai'-te.

ကော်ဖီအေး ကြိုက်တယ်။

[He] likes cold coffee.

13.   thu sa:-da mya:-de.
          သူ စားတာ များတယ်။
          He eats a lot.

14.   A: bai'-hsa-bi-la:?
          ဗိုက်ဆာပြီလား။
          Are you hungry?

      B: thei' hsa-de.
          သိပ် ဆာတယ်။
          [I am] very hungry.

      C: mə-ho'-hpu:. bai'-mə-hsa-bu:.
          မဟုတ်ဘူး။ ဗိုက်မဆာဘူး။
          No. I'm not hungry.

15.   A: thụ-go sauṇ-da hnə'-na-yi shị-bi.
          သူ့ကို စောင့်တာ နှစ်နာရီ ရှိပြီ။
          I have been waiting for him for two hours.

      B: thụ-go mə-hma'-mi-bu:.
          သူ့ကို မမှတ်မိဘူး။
          I don't recognize him.

16.   sa-o'-twei hpa'-bọ we-de.
          စာအုပ်တွေ ဖတ်ဖို့ ဝယ်တယ်။
          I buy books for reading.

17.   yei-nwe: pei:-ba.
          ရေနွေး ပေးပါ။
          Bring some tea, please.

18.   ə-sa' shọ-ba.
          အစပ် လျှော့ပါ။
          Make it less spicy, please.

19.   ə-ngan shɔ̞-ba.

အငန် လျှော့ပါ။

Less salty, please.

Drills

1. Practice saying the following sentences in Myanmar. If the sentence is a question, practice answering it as well.

I have too many books.

_____

What foods do you like to eat?

_____

Have you ever visited Mandalay?

_____

Why do you use chopsticks?

_____

She drinks bottled water, but she does not drink tap water.

_____

2. Do the following.

Create a dialogue asking someone what kind of food they like. Ask that person why they like it and have the person give an answer (because it's sweet, delicious, etc.)

Compose a short telephone conversation between two people that has each of the following parts: an opening greeting, asking if the person is home, and asking the receiver of the call if he or she wants to do something with the caller.

3. Use the following words to form ten sentences.

zei: ဈေး	ta'-te တတ်တယ်	htə-min:-zain ထမင်းဆိုင်
ə-me: အမဲ	ngan-de ငန်တယ်	mə-tain-mi မတိုင်မီ
ho-hma ဟိုမှာ	jə-ma̱ ကျွန်မ	ə-thi: အသီး
yei ရေ	jai'-te ကြိုက်တယ်	yei-than̠ ရေသန့်
mə-nei̠-ga̱ မနေ့က	au' အောက်	ə-yə-dha shi̠-de အရသာ ရှိတယ်
zun: ဇွန်း	je' ကြက်	-tho' သုပ်
chin-de ချဉ်တယ်	tu တူ	mei'-hswei မိတ်ဆွေ
da: ဓား	cho-de ချိုတယ်	dhə-gaun သန်းခေါင်
sa'-te စပ်တယ်	ə-yan: အရမ်း	hsain-ge ဆိုင်ကယ်
we' ဝက်	hin:-jo ဟင်းချို	da-ba-be: ဒါပါပဲ
wa̱-bi ဝပြီ	thei' သိပ်	htə-min:jɔ ထမင်းကြော်

Test 7

Match the English words with the Burmese words.

_____ 1. to be bitter   a. wa̤-bi ဝပြီ

_____ 2. fish   b. cho-de ချိုတယ်

_____ 3. to be sour   c. ə-me: အမဲ

_____ 4. delicious   d. zun: ဇွန်း

_____ 5. food   e. ngan-de ငန်တယ်

_____ 6. to be salty   f. hka:-de ခါးတယ်

_____ 7. beef   g. sa'-te စပ်တယ်

_____ 8. spoon   h. nga: ငါး

_____ 9. to be hungry   i. da: ဓား

_____ 10. knife   j. bai'-hsa-de ဗိုက်ဆာတယ်

_____ 11. fork   k. chin-de ချဉ်တယ်

_____ 12. to be spicy   l. hkə-yin: ခက်ရင်း

                               m. ə-sa:-ə-sa အစားအစာ

                               n. ə-yə-dha shḭ-de အရသာ ရှိတယ်

Translate the following into English or Burmese.

1. မြန်မာအစားအစာ ကြိုက်တယ် ဒါပေမဲ့ ဗီယက်နမ်အစားအစာ မကြိုက်ဘူး။

_____

2. မစိုးစိုး အိမ်မှာလား။

_____

3. မြန်မာဟင်း သိပ် မစပ်ဘူး။

_____

4. This soup is very salty. I can't eat it.

_____

5. Have you ever eaten Shan noodles?

_____

Reading & Writing

Weakening

Another important factor in Burmese pronunciation is called "weakening", which is the way a vowel is sometimes shortened into a shwa (ə). This sound is found in the English words th*e*, *a*bout and *a*round. Weakening also occurs in English, such as when "going to" and "want to" are pronounced as "gonna" and "wanna". Perhaps the most common cases in Burmese are the words that combine the numbers one (ti' တစ်), two (hni' နှစ်) and seven (hkun-ni' ခုနှစ်) with another word:

one litre	tə-li-ta	တစ်လီတာ
one mile	tə-main	တစ်မိုင်
two hours	hnə-na-yi	နှစ်နာရီ
two million	hnə-than:	နှစ်သန်း
two cups	hnə-hkwe'	နှစ်ခွက်
seven hours	hkun-hnə-na-yi	ခုနှစ်နာရီ

Some other words are also weakened such as the words thu သူ nga: ငါး and sa စာ. The following list gives examples of other weakened words in Burmese:

ငါး

shark	ngə-man:	ငါးမန်း
flying fish	ngə-pyan	ငါးပျံ
fish cake/ball	ngə-hso'	ငါးဆုပ်

စာ

| clerk | sə-yei: | စာရေး |
| list | sə-yin: | စာရင်း |

သား

first born	thə-u:	သားဦး
leather	thə-yei	သားရေ
womb	thə-ein	သားအိမ်

သူ

hero, warrior	thə-ye:	သူရဲ
child	thə-nge	သူငယ်
thief	thə-hko:	သူခိုး

ကုလား: (meaning Indian)

| chair | kə-lə-htain | ကုလားထိုင် |
| camel | kə-lə-o' | ကုလားအုတ် |

Writing Exercise 7

Transliterate the following sentences in Burmese and mark *all* cases of weakened consonants (Note: please review the words in the irregularly pronounced words section of Lesson 9 for this exercise).

1. One thousand two hundred kyats.

2. He wants to sit in the leather chair.

3. Waiter, do you have shark soup today?.

4. It takes two hours to [go to] Bago by bus.

5. Bananas and fish paste are on the table.

6. I want to eat a serving of shrimp curry.

7. Ko Tun Moe (htun: mo:) comes from Bhamo. He is twenty years old.

8. Ananda Pahto is in Bagan.

Lesson 8

body parts and health issues; commands; gender and plural forms; ordinal numbers; stacked consonants

thin-gan:-za shi'   သင်ခန်းစာ ၈   **Lesson 8**
wɔ:-ha-rạ   ဝေါဟာရ   **Vocabulary**

Nouns

ko	ကိုယ်	body
gaun:	ခေါင်း	head
zə-bin	ဆံပင်	hair
mye'-hna	မျက်နှာ	face
mye'-sị	မျက်စိ	eye
mye'-hkon:	မျက်ခုံး	eyebrow
mye'-taun	မျက်တောင်	eyelash
hnə-gaun:	နှာခေါင်း	nose
bə-za'	ပါးစပ်	mouth
hnə-hkan:-mwei:	နှုတ်ခမ်းမွေး	mustache
mei:	မေး	chin
hnə-hkan:	နှုတ်ခမ်း	lips
sha	လျှာ	tongue
thwa:	သွား	tooth
na:	နား	ear
le-bin:	လည်ပင်း	neck
le-jaun:	လည်ချောင်း	throat
yin-ba'	ရင်ဘတ်	chest
jɔ:-gon:	ကျောကုန်း	back

hka:	ခါး	waist, lower back
ə-sa-ein	အစာအိမ်	stomach
le'	လက်	arm, hand
le'-hpə-wa:	လက်ဖဝါး	palm
le'-chaun:	လက်ချောင်း	finger
le'-the:	လက်သည်း	fingernail
pə-hkon:	ပခုံး	shoulder
chei	ခြေ	leg
chei-hta'	ခြေထောက်	foot
chei-bə-wa:	ခြေဖဝါး	sole of the foot
chei-jaun:	ခြေချောင်း	toe
du:	ဒူး	knee
paun	ပေါင်	thigh
ə-yei-bya:	အရေပြား	skin
on:-hnau'	ဦးနှောက်	brain
hnə-lon:	နှလုံး	heart
ə-hso'	အဆုတ်	lung
ə-the:	အသည်း	liver
jwe'-tha	ကြွက်သား	muscle
ə-yo:	အရိုး	bone
ə-hpya:	အဖျား	fever
hsə-ya-wun	ဆရာဝန်	doctor
hsei:	ဆေး	medicine

ə-wu'-ə-sa:	အဝတ်အစား	clothing
ə-nwei:-hte	အနွေးထည်	warm clothes
in:-ji	အကျႌ	shirt
tai'-pon	တိုက်ပုံ	jacket, coat
baun:-bi	ဘောင်းဘီ	pants, trousers
sə-ka'	စကတ်	skirt
o'-hto'	ဦးထုပ်	hat
hpə-na'	ဖိနပ်	shoes
chei-ei'	ခြေအိတ်	stockings
le'-ei'	လက်အိတ်	gloves
hka:-ba'	ခါးပတ်	belt
le'-swu'	လက်စွပ်	ring
le'-kau'	လက်ကောက်	bracelet
hsa'-pya	ဆပ်ပြာ	soap
thaṇ	သန့်	clean
bə-gan	ပန်းကန်	dishes
ə-chein-mi	အချိန်မီ	in time, on time (adv)
ba-hmạ	ဘာမှ	nothing
ə-thi'	အသစ်	new
ə-haun:	အဟောင်း	old (thing)

Verbs

na-de	နာတယ်	to hurt, be in pain
nei-kaun:-de	နေကောင်းတယ်	to feel well
nei-mə-kaun:-bu:	နေမကောင်းဘူး။	"[I] am not well."
ə-ei:-mị-de	အအေးမိတယ်	to have a cold
ə-the:-gwe:-de	အသည်းကွဲတယ်	to be heartbroken (lit., 'split livered')
wu'-hta:-te	ဝတ်ထားတယ်	to wear (clothes)
hsaun:-de	ဆောင်းတယ်	to wear (a hat)
si:-de	စီးတယ်	to wear (shoes)
cho'-te	ချွတ်တယ်	to remove
ə-wu' shɔ-de	အဝတ် လျှော်တယ်	to wash clothes, do laundry
gaun:-hpi:-de	ခေါင်းဖြီးတယ်	to comb hair
yei'-te	ရိတ်တယ်	to shave
thwa:-tai'-te	သွားတိုက်တယ်	to brush teeth
yei-cho:-de	ရေချိုးတယ်	to bathe/ wash one's self
shɔ-de	လျှော်တယ်	to wash (clothes)
gaun: shɔ-de	ခေါင်း လျှော်တယ်	to wash one's hair (lit., wash head)
le' hsei:-de	လက် ဆေးတယ်	to wash hands
bə-gan hsei:-de	ပန်းကန် ဆေးတယ်	to wash dishes
lo-de	လိုတယ်	to need

lo-a'-te	လိုအပ်တယ်	to need, want something
gaun:-kai'-te	ခေါင်းကိုက်တယ်	to have a headache
bai'-na-de	ဗိုက်နာတယ်	to have stomach ache
wun:-shɔ-de	ဝမ်းလျှောတယ်	to have diarrhea
the'-tha-de	သက်သာတယ်	to feel better, recover
hlạ-de	လှတယ်	to be pretty, beautiful
thei:	သေး	still
mə-...-thei:-bu:	မ...သေးဘူး	not yet [+ verb]
nau'-jạ-de	နောက်ကျတယ်	to be late

Ordinal Numbers

pə-htə-mạ	ပထမ	first
dụ-tị-yạ	ဒုတိယ	second
tạ-tị-yạ	တတိယ	third
zə-do'-htạ	စတုတ္ထ	fourth
pyin-zə-mạ	ပဉ္စမ	fifth
hsa'-htə-mạ	ဆဋ္ဌမ	sixth
tha'-tə-mạ	သတ္တမ	seventh
a'-htə-mạ	အဋ္ဌမ	eighth
nə-wə-mạ	နဝမ	ninth
dạ-thə-mạ	ဒသမ	tenth

thə-da   သဒ္ဒါ   **Grammar**

Command form of a verb

The command form of verbs in Burmese is simply formed by using
the root of a verb:

Sit!	htain!	ထိုင်။
Come here!	di-go la!	ဒီကို လာ။

The pa/ba particle can be included to be more polite. Thus, the
following examples is more typical of spoken Burmese:

Please Sit!	htain-ba	ထိုင်ပါ။

In some cases the particle -gẹ ခဲ့ may be included in the command
form of a verb. It has a similar function as the noun particle -hsi
ဆီ. A case of this is for the verb "come", for which you may
commonly hear:

Come [to me]! la-gẹ!		လာခဲ့။

Finally, another common way of added the idea that some action is
obligatory is to add the final particle yạ ရ. A common sign would
be:

No smoking.	hsei:-lei' mə-thau'-yạ	ဆေးလိပ် မသောက်ရ။

(Note also that since this is an example of a negative command, the
-hpu:/bu: particle is replaced with yạ)

Noun Particles: -ma ⊌, -thu/dhu သူ, -tha:/dha သား: (Gender)

Gender-based forms of nouns do sometimes exist in Burmese and are indicated by adding a suffix to a noun. In some cases, the masculine form has no suffix. The feminine form, when it exists, uses the suffix -ma (⊌). A very common example is found in the word for teacher:

| teacher (m) | hsə-ya | ဆရာ |
| teacher (f) | hsə-ya-ma | ဆရာမ |

Animal and plant names also generally have male and female forms (though not always). For example, the suffix -hti:/di: (ထီး) is sometimes used for females and -hpo (ဖို) or -hpa (ဖ) for males. Here are two examples:

tiger	ja:	ကျား:
tigress	ja:-ma	ကျား:မ
male tiger	ja:-di:	ကျား:ထီး
chicken	je'	ကြက်
hen	je'-ma	ကြက်မ
rooster, cock	je'-hpa	ကြက်ဖ

Noun Particle: -twe/dwe ေတြ , -to/do တို့ (Plural form)

There is a plural form in Burmese, though it is often left out. Also,
unlike English, the plural form is not used for proper nouns or
numbers. There are two forms. Generally, the plural form is shown
by adding the suffix -dwei (ေတြ). For example:

| person | lu | လူ |
| people | lu-dwei | လူေတြ |

For pronouns, the suffix -to/do (တို့) is used instead, as in:

| He/she | thu | သူ |
| they | thu-do | သူတို့ |

This case also be used in the possessive form:

| our car | do-ka: | တို့ကား |

or to indicate a group of people associated with the subject:

Ma Sein and her family (or friends)
ma-sein-do   မစိန်တို့

Conversation

George nei-kaun:-la: ma̱-sein?

ကျော်ချီ နေကောင်းလား မစိန်။

How are you doing, Ma Sein?

Sein nei-mə-kaun:-bu:.

စိန် နေမကောင်းဘူး။

[I'm] not well.

George ba hpyi'-ta-le:?

ကျော်ချီ ဘာ ဖြစ်တာလဲ။

What's the matter?

Sein le-jaun: na-de.

စိန် လည်ချောင်း နာတယ်။

My throat hurts.

George hpya:-la:?

ကျော်ချီ ဖျားလား။

Do you have a temperature?

Sein hpya:-de.

စိန် ဖျားတယ်။

[Yes, I] have a fever.

George	o, mə-kaun:-bu:. hsei: thau'-pi:-bi-la:?
ကျော်ချို	အို၊ မကောင်းဘူး။ ဆေး သောက်ပြီးပြီလား။
	Oh, that's not good. Have you taken any medicine?

Sein	hiṇ-in:, ba-hmạ mə-thau'-thei:-bu:.
စိန်	ဟင့်အင်း၊ ဘာမှ မသောက်သေးဘူး။
	No, I haven't taken anything yet.

George	hsei: thau'-ba. ə-na:-yu-ba.
ကျော်ချို	ဆေး သောက်ပါ။ အနားယူပါ။
	Please take some medicine and rest.

Sein	ho'-kẹ. lo'-me. nau'-hmạ twei̯-me.
စိန်	ဟုတ်ကဲ့။ လုပ်မယ်။ နောက်မှ တွေ့မယ်။
	Okay. I'll do that. See you later.

wa-ja̱-mya: ဝါကျများ   **Sentences**

1. A: ba lo'-hpo̱ shi̱-le:?
       ဘာ လုပ်ဖို့ ရှိလဲ။
       What do you need to do?

   B: sa'-o' hpa'-hpo̱ shi̱-de.
       စာအုပ် ဖတ်ဖို့ ရှိတယ်။
       I need to read a book.

   C: hnə'-na-yi-hma zei: thwa:-bo̱ shi̱-de.
       နှစ်နာရီမှာ ဈေး သွားဖို့ ရှိတယ်။
       I need to go to the market at 2:00.

2. A: ba-lo-le:?
       ဘာလိုလဲ။
       What do you need?

   B: mɔ-tɔ-hsain-ge ə-thi' lo-de.
       မော်တော်ဆိုင်ကယ် အသစ် လိုတယ်။
       I need a new motorbike.

   C: zun:-ne̱ hkə-yin: lo-de.
       ဇွန်း နဲ့ ခက်ရင်း လိုတယ်။
       I need a spoon and fork.

3. A: thu ə-wu' shɔ-pi:-bi-la:?
       သူ အဝတ် လျှော်ပြီးပြီလား။
       Has he done the laundry yet?

B: hiṇ-in:, mə-pi:-thei:-bu:.
ဟင့်အင်း၊ မပြီးသေးဘူး။
No, its not finished yet.

C: pi:-bi.
ပြီးပြီ။
[Its] already done.

4. A: thu yau'-pi-la:?
သူ ရောက်ပြီလား။
Has he arrived yet?

B: ho'-kẹ, thu yau'-pi:-bi.
ဟုတ်ကဲ့၊ သူ ရောက်ပြီးပြီ။
Yes, he has arrived already.

C: hiṇ-in:, thu mə-yau'-thei:-bu:.
ဟင့်အင်း၊ သူ မရောက်သေးဘူး။
No, he hasn't arrived yet.

5. A: bə-gan ə-chein-mi hsei:-pi:-bi-la:?
ပန်းကန် အချိန်မီ ဆေးပြီးပြီလား။
Did you wash the dishes in time?

B: ho'-kẹ, hsei:-pi:-bi.
ဟုတ်ကဲ့၊ ဆေးပြီးပြီ။
Yes, [they're] already washed.

C: hiṇ-in:, mə-hsei:-yạ-thei:-bu:.
ဟင့်အင်း၊ မဆေးရသေးဘူး။
No, [they] haven't been washed yet.

6.   A: ə-chein-mi yau'-la:?
          အချိန်မီ ရောက်လား။
          Did [you] arrive in time?

     B: ho'-kɛ, ə-chein-mi yau'-te.
          ဟုတ်ကဲ့၊ အချိန်မီ ရောက်တယ်။
          Yes, [I] arrived in time.

     C: hin-in:, ə-chein-mi mə-yau'-hpu:.
          ဟင့်အင်း၊ အချိန်မီ မရောက်ဘူး။
          No, [I] didn't arrive on time.

7.   A: thu ba-wu'-hta:-le:?
          သူ ဘာဝတ်ထားလဲ။
          What is she wearing?

     B: thu sə-ka' ə-pya-nɛ in:-ji ə-hpyu wu'-hta:-de.
          သူ စကတ် အပြာနဲ့ အကျႌ အဖြူ ဝတ်ထားတယ်။
          She is wearing a blue skirt and a white shirt.

     C: baun:-bi ə-ne' wu'-hta:-de.
          ဘောင်းဘီ အနက် ဝတ်ထားတယ်။
          [She is] wearing black pants.

     D: in:-ji ə-ni wu'-hta:-de.
          အကျႌ အနီ ဝတ်ထားတယ်။
          [She is] wearing a red shirt.

8.   A: nei-kaun:-la:?
          နေကောင်းလား။
          Are you feeling well?

B: nei-kaun:-ba-de.
      နေကောင်းပါတယ်။
      [I'm] feeling fine.

C: nei-mə-kaun:-bu:.
      နေမကောင်းဘူး။
      [I am] not feeling well.

D: gaun:-kai'-te.
      ခေါင်းကိုက်တယ်။
      [I] have a headache.

E: bai'-na-de.
      ဗိုက်နာတယ်။
      [I] have a stomach ache. (lit. "stomach hurts")

F: wun:-shɔ-de.
      ဝမ်းလျှောတယ်။
      [I] have diarrhea.

9.   A.   hpə-na' si:-lọ yạ-mə-la:.
            ဖိနပ် စီးလို့ ရမလား။
            May I wear shoes?

      B.   hpə-na' si:-lọ yạ-de.
            ဖိနပ် စီးလို့ ရတယ်။
            You can wear shoes.

      C.   hpə-na' si:-lọ mə-yạ-bu:.
            ဖိနပ် စီးလို့ မရဘူး။
            No, you can't wear shoes.

Drills

1. Practice saying the following sentences in Myanmar. If the sentence is a question, practice answering it as well.

I have to go to the bathrom.

_____

Did Bob wash the dishes yet?

_____

2. Fill in the blanks in the diagram below with the Burmese word for each body part.

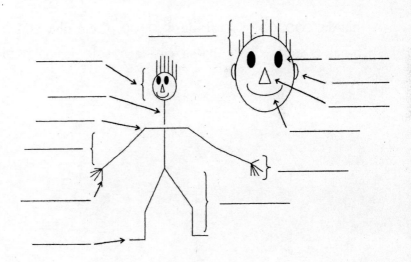

3. Use the following words to form ten sentences.

bə-gan ပန်းကန်
mə-tain-mi မတိုင်မီ
ein အိမ်
sa'-te စပ်တယ်
sə-ka' စကတ်
ə-wu' အဝတ်
gaun: ခေါင်း
in:-ji အင်္ကျီ
-la:? လား

hlạ-de လှတယ်
ə-na: အနား

na-de နာတယ်
-hma မှာ
ə-yaun အရောင်
we-de ဝယ်တယ်
o'-hto' ဦးထုပ်
wu'-te ဝတ်တယ်
hke' ခက်
thu သူ
ei'-de အိပ်တယ်

si:-de စီးတယ်
ba/pa ပါ

ə-chein-mi အချိန်မီ
thə-be'-hka သန်ဘက်ခါ
ə-thi' အသစ်
le'-su' လက်စွပ်
hsa'-pya ဆပ်ပြာ
ə-sa-ein အစားအိမ်
hpə-na' ဖိနပ်
hkə-mya: ခင်ဗျား
mə-pi:-thei:-bu: မပြီးသေးဘူး

ein-dha အိမ်သာ
lo-de လိုတယ်

Test 8

Match the English words with the Burmese words.

_____ 1. clothes   a. le' လက်

_____ 2. new   b. sə-ka' စကတ်

_____ 3. skirt   c. in:-ji အင်္ကျီ

_____ 4. face   d. ə-wu'-ə-sa: အဝတ်အစား

_____ 5. body   e. mye'-si̥ မျက်စိ

_____ 6. to wash   f. ko ကိုယ်

_____ 7. arm   g. mye'-hna မျက်နှာ

_____ 8. eyes   h. on:-nhau' ဦးနှောက်

_____ 9. medicine   i. hnə-lon: နှလုံး

_____ 10. brain   j. bə-za' ပါးစပ်

_____ 11. shirt   k. hsei: ဆေး

_____ 12. mouth   l. shɔ-de လျှော်တယ်

     m. ə-thi' အသစ်

Translate the following into English or Myanmar.

1. ဘုရားမှာ ဖိနပ် စီးလို့ မရဘူး။

_____

2. သူ အက်ိုို အဖြူနဲ့ ဘောင်းဘီ အပြာ ဝတ်ထားတယ်။

_____

3. ကျွန်တော် ဝမ်းလျှောတယ်။ ခေါင်းလည်း ကိုက်တယ်။

_____

4. I need new clothes.

_____

5. His hat is very big.

_____

Reading & Writing

Stacked Consonants

Anyone reading Myanmar will occasionally see two consonants written one on top of the other. These "stack consonants" are a Burmese form of contraction rather like the way we write "don't" or "can't" in English. Words with stacked consonants can be tricky to pronounce because most of these words come from Pali and also because something gets deleted to form the contraction. For example,

take a look at the Myanmar word for world: ကမ္ဘာ pronounced: gə-ba

If uncontracted, this word would be written: ကမ်ဘာ

ကမ္ဘာ demonstrates the three main features of stacked consonants.
1) the second consonant is placed underneath the first.
2) any symbol written above the first consonant is removed (almost always a killer stroke).
3) if a vowel symbol remains it is now placed over or next to the upper consonant, but it is still understood to modify the lower consonant. For example, the yẹ-cha (ာ) in ကမ္ဘာ modifies the lower consonant (ဘ) rather than the upper (မ)[29].

---

[29] Note that this example is also a special case of weakening in which the nasal n at the end of the first syllable is not pronounced.

Below are some additional examples of Myanmar words with stacked consonants:

Word	Pronounced As	Translation
ကမ္ဘာ	gə-ba	world
ကိစ္စ	kei'-sa	matter, issue
ကုမ္ပဏီ	kon-bə-ni	company
ကြမ္မာ	jam-ma	fortune
စက္ကူ	se'-ku	paper
တိရစ္ဆာန်	tə-rei'-hsan	animal
ဓမ္မ	də-ma̱	teachings of the Buddha
ပိန္နဲသီး	pein:-ne:-dhi:	jack fruit
ပတ္တမြား	bə-də-hmya:	ruby
မဂ္ဂဇင်း	me'-gə-zin:	magazine
မန္တလေး	man:-də-lei:	Mandalay
သတ္တိ	tha'-thi	courage
သဒ္ဒါ	thə-da	grammar
သမ္မတ	thə-mə-da̱	president
ဝတ္ထု	wu'-hto	novel, story
အက္ခရာ	e'-hkə-ya	character, script
အာဂန္တု	a-gan-du	visiting monk
အန္တရာယ်	an-də-ye	danger
အိန္ဒိယ	ein-di̱-ya̱	India
ဥက္ကာပျံ	o'-ka-byan	shooting star

Writing Exercise 8

Translate the following sentences into Burmese.

1. He studies at Yangon University.

2. We're going the to the World Famous Teashop. Will you follow?

3. It doesn't matter.

4. I want to go to the zoo tomorrow.

5. We usually eat jackfruit in the rainy season.

6. He works for a Japanese company.

7. Next month I will go to Mandalay.

8. Do you have a 200 kyat bill?

Lesson 9

classifiers; comparisons; traveller's needs; rarely
used consonants and symbols; shopping for clothes

thin-gan:-za ko: သင်ခန်းစာ ၉   Lesson 9
wɔ.-ha-ṛa   ဝေါဟာရ   Vocabulary

Nouns

ə-myo:-dha:	အမျိုးသား	husband, boyfriend, gentleman, man
ə-myo:-dhə-mi:	အမျိုးသမီး	girlfriend, lady, woman
ə-lei:-chein	အလေးချိန်	weight

Verbs

pu-de	ပူတယ်	to be hot
pu-de-nɔ?	ပူတယ်နော်။	"It's hot, isn't it?"
ei:-de	အေးတယ်	to be cool or cold
pein-de	ပိန်တယ်	to be skinny
htu-de	ထူတယ်	to be thick
pa:-de	ပါးတယ်	to be thin, light
lei:-de	လေးတယ်	to be heavy
pɔ-de	ပေါ့တယ်	to be light, not heavy
myin-de	မြင့်တယ်	to be tall; high
than-de	သန်တယ်	to be strong, healthy
a:-ne:-de	အားနည်းတယ်	to be weak
tau'-te	တောက်တယ်	to be bright, brilliant (color)
hmaun-de	မှောင်တယ်	to be dark
pyin:-de	ပျင်းတယ်	to be lazy, be bored
pya:-de	ပြားတယ်	to be flat, to be flattened
chau'-te	ခြောက်တယ်	to be dry
so-de	စိုတယ်	to be wet

nyi'-pa'-te	ညစ်ပတ်တယ်	to be dirty
chan:-dha-de	ချမ်းသာတယ်	to be rich
hsin:-ye:-de	ဆင်းရဲတယ်	to be poor
cho:-de	ချိုးတယ်	to break
ə-tu-du	အတူတူ	to be the same, similar
ə-tu-du-be:.	အတူတူပဲ။	"They are the same."
mə-tu-bu:.	မတူဘူး။	"They are not the same."
po-de	ပိုတယ်	to be more than

Particles

-hte'	ထက်	more than, greater than
-hson:/zon:	ဆုံး	most, greatest
ə-ɟi:-hson:-be:.	အကြီးဆုံးပဲ။	The biggest one.
ə-twe'	အတွက်	for

Traveller's Needs

mi:-ɟi'	မီးခြစ်	matches, lighter
da'-hke:	ဓာတ်ခဲ	battery (dry cell, e.g., flashlight batteries)
be'-htri	ဘက်ထရီ	battery (wet cell, e.g, car batteries)
hpə-yaun:-dain	ဖယောင်းတိုင်	candle
da'-mi:	ဓါတ်မီး	flashlight, torch
thwa:-tai'-hsei:	သွားတိုက်ဆေး	toothpaste
chin-zei:-gwei	ခြင်ဆေးခွေ	mosquito coil
hsa'-pya	ဆပ်ပြာ	soap
gaun:-shɔ-ye	ခေါင်းလျှော်ရည်	shampoo

thə-da   သဒ္ဒါ   **Grammar**

Classifying Nouns

Classifiers (also called counting nouns or counters) are sometimes used in English, as in: "four *cups* of tea", "a *bunch* of grapes" or "three *pairs* of socks". In Burmese, however, classifiers are almost always included whenever a noun is quantified. Also, while the English pattern is: quantity, classifier, noun; the word order in Burmese is: noun, quantity, classifier. Note that there are two classifiers for bottles, depending on whether or not the bottle is glass or plastic and that the counter for a cup is different from the counter for a "cup-sized serving". Here are some examples:

a cup	hkwe' tə-lon:	ခွက် တစ်လုံး
a cup of coffee	kɔ-hpi tə-hkwe'	ကော်ဖီ တစ်ခွက်
a (glass) bottle of beer	bi-ya:- tə-lon:	ဘီယာ တစ်လုံး
2 (plastic) bottles of water	yei-than hnə-bu:	ရေသန့် နှစ်ဘူး
5 books	sa-o' nga:-o'	စာအုပ် ငါးအုပ်

A related term that comes in handy is lau' (လောက်) meaning "about". For example:

About 50 people   nga:-ze yau' lau'   ငါးဆယ် ယောက် လောက်

Below is a list of some of the most common classifiers in Burmese.

people	yau'	ယောက်
day(s)	ye'	ရက်
animals	kaun/gaun	ကောင်
round things, fruit, glass bottles	lon:	လုံး
plates, mats, mirrors	cha'/ja'	ချပ်

sheets of paper, leaves, doors	ywe'	ရွက်
cigarettes, cheroots, rolls of film or tissue	lei'	လိပ်
letters, newspapers, magazines, tickets	saun	စောင်
bunches ("branch") of fruit, flowers	hkain/gain	ခိုင်
glass or cup of water, tea, etc.	hkwe'/gwe'	ခွက်
servings, bowls of a dish	pwe:/bwe:	ပွဲ
clothing, cloth articles (such as blankets)	hte/de	ထည်
vehicles, animals that can be ridden	si:/zi:	စီး
houses	ein	အိမ်
floors of a building	hta'	ထပ်
musical instruments, tools, weapons, umbrellas	le'	လက်
rod-like objects (needles, pencils, knives, spoons, fingers, toes, arms and legs)	chaun:/jaun:	ချောင်း
boxes, cans, tins, plastic containers, plastic bottles	bu:	ဘူး
"generic" counter	hku/gu	ခု

Comparisons

Being able to compare two things is an important skill in any language. Here we'll discuss four kinds of comparisons: simple comparisons ("A is more than B"), implied comparisons ("the bigger one"), superlatives ("the biggest one") and equalities (A is the same as B). The examples below and sample sentences presented in this lesson will help you develop this ability in Burmese.

Noun Particle: -hte/de ထက် (more than, used in simple comparisons)

Simple comparisons in Burmese use the particles -hte' (ထက်), a suffix added to the end of the noun being compared.
For example:

"That house is bigger than this house."

would be

ho-ein-ga̱ di-ein-hte' ji:-de   ဟိုအိမ်က ဒီအိမ်ထက် ကြီးတယ်။
(literally: that house/this house-than/more-big-is).
Another example would be:

Ko Moe is taller than Ko Sein.
ko-mo:-ga̱ ko-sein-hte' myin-de. ကိုမိုးက ကိုစိန်ထက် မြင့်တယ်။
(literally: ko mo-from/ko sein-more than/tall-is)

Verb: -po ပို (more than, used in implied comparisons)

The way to make an implied comparison is by using the verb po ပို, meaning to be more than and combining it with the verb used in the comparison, making it possible to say something is better, prettier, etc. than something else without mentioning the object of the comparison. For example:

"the prettier blouse"   in:-ji:po-hla̱-de.   အက်ျို ပိုလှတယ်။

Or simply:

"the prettier one" po-hla̱-de.   ပိုလှတယ်။

Noun Particle: -hson/zon ဆုံး (most, best)

To say something is the best or the prettiest, etc., use the suffix hson: (ဆုံး) as follows:

That is the best one.   da ə-kaun:-hson:-be:.   ဒါ အကောင်းဆုံးပါ။

Or more simply: "the prettiest [one]"   ə-hla̱-hson: အလှဆုံး

To say something is "the worst" ("most bad") is:

"the worst [one]" ə-hso:-hson: အဆိုးဆုံး

Noun: ə-tu-du အတူတူ (used to say two things are the same)

To say that something or someone is the same as something else, use the phrase:

"They are the same."   ə-tu-du-be:. အတူတူပဲ။

To more clearly show two things are the same, use the particles -ga̱ (က) and ne̱ (နဲ့) with ə-tu-du-be: (အတူတူပဲ). For example:

Nanda and Min are the same age.
ma̱-nan-da-ne̱ ko-min:-ga̱ ə-the' ə-tu-du-be:.
မနန္ဒာနဲ့ ကိုမင်းက အသက် အတူတူပဲ။
(literally: Nanda-and/Min age/the same as)

To say something is "about the same" as something else add lau' (လောက်) before pe:/be: (ပဲ):

[She's] about the same age.
ə-the' ə-tu-du-lau'-pe.   အသက် အတူတူလောက်ပဲ။

Finally, to say something is "not the same" as something else, say:

"not the same"   mə-tu-bu: မတူဘူး

Conversation

Salesperson: ရောင်းသူ	ba lo-jin-dhə-le:? ဘာ လိုချင်သလဲ။ What would you like?
Customer: ဝယ်သူ	htə-mein shị-dhə-la:? ထဘီ ရှိသလား။ Do you have longyis[30]?.
Salesperson: ရောင်းသူ	shị-de. ba ə-yaun jai'-thə-le:? ရှိတယ်။ ဘာ အရောင် ကြိုက်သလဲ။ [Yes, we] do. What colors do you like?
Customer: ဝယ်သူ	ə-pya-nẹ ə-sein:, shị-la:? အပြာနဲ့ အစိမ်း ရှိလား။ Do you have blue and green?
Salesperson: ရောင်းသူ	shị-de. di htə-mein jai'-thə-la:? ရှိတယ်။ ဒီ ထဘီ ကြိုက်သလား။ [Yes, we] do. Do you like this one?
Customer: ဝယ်သူ	jai'-te. be-lau'-le:? ကြိုက်တယ်။ ဘယ်လောက်လဲ။ Yes, I like it. How much is it?
Salesperson: ရောင်းသူ	nga:-daun, shin. ငါးထောင် ရှင်။ Five thousand, sir.

---

[30] htə-mein (ထဘီ but note this word isn't pronounced the way it's written) is a woman's longyi.

Customer: zei:-mya:-de. shɔ-ba-on:, dɔ-lei:?
ဝယ်သူ   ဈေးများတယ်။ လျှော့ပါဦး ဒေါ်လေး။
                    That's a lot. Can you lower the price, auntie?

Salesperson: be-hnə-hte yu-hma-le:?
ရောင်းသူ   ဘယ်နှစ်ထည် ယူမှာလဲ။
                    How many longyis will you buy?

Customer: thon:-de.
ဝယ်သူ   သုံးထည်။
                    Three (pieces).

Salesperson: e:-da-hso, lei:-daun nga:-ya-nẹ yu-ba.
ရောင်းသူ   အဲဒါဆို၊ လေးထောင့် ငါးရာနဲ့ ယူပါ။
                    In that case, I can take forty-five hundred for
                    them.

Customer: yu-me.
ဝယ်သူ   ယူမယ်။
                    [Okay], I'll take them.

Salesperson: da be:-la:? tə-cha: ba-lo-jin-dhə-le:?
ရောင်းသူ   ဒါပဲလား။ တခြား ဘာလိုချင်သလဲ။
                    Is that everything? What else would you like?

Customer: nyi-mạ-lei: ə-twe' in:-ji tə-hte lo-jin-de.
                    le'-to in:-ji shị-la:?
ဝယ်သူ   ညီမလေး အတွက် အက်ျီ တစ်ထည်
                    လိုချင်တယ်။ လက်တို အက်ျီ ရှိလား။
                    [Yes], I want to buy a blouse for my younger
                    sister.
                    Do you have any with short sleeves?

Salesperson: ရောင်းသူ	shị-de. di in:-ɟi jai'-thə-la:? ရှိတယ်။ ဒီ အင်္ကျီ ကြိုက်သလား။ We do! Do you like this blouse?
Customer: ဝယ်သူ	o, hlạ-de, tə-cha: ə-yaun shị-thei:-la:?. အို၊ လှတယ်၊ တစ်ခြား အရောင် ရှိသေးလား။ Oh, that's beautiful, do you have another color?.
Salesperson: ရောင်းသူ	ə-yaun ə-mya:-ji: shị-de.. အရောင် အများကြီး ရှိတယ်။ [We have] many colors here.
Customer: ဝယ်သူ	a-pyu yu-me. be-lau'-le:? အဖြူ ယူမယ်။ ဘယ်လောက်လဲ။ I'll take the white one. How much is it?
Salesperson: ရောင်းသူ	thon:-daun-ba. သုံးထောင်ပါ။ Three thousand, please.
Customer: ဝယ်သူ	kaun:-de. yu-me. ကောင်းတယ်၊ ယူမယ်။ Good, I'll take it.
Salesperson: ရောင်းသူ	jei:-zu:-be:. nau'-tə-hka la-gẹ-nɔ? ကျေးဇူးပဲ။ နောက်တစ်ခါ လာခဲ့နော်။ Thanks. Next time, come again, okay?

wa-ja̱-mya: ဝါကျများ:   **Sentences**

1. A: hpə-na' ə-me:-ga̱ ə-pyu-hte' hla̱-de.

   ဘိနပ် အမည်းက အဖြူထက် လှတယ်။

   The black shoes are prettier than the white shoes.

   B: hpə-na' ə-me:-ga̱ ə-ni-hte' mə-hla̱-bu:.

   ဘိနပ် အမည်းက အနီထက် မလှဘူး။

   The black shoes are not prettier than the red shoes.

   C: hpə-na' ə-me:-ga̱ ə-hla̱-hson:-be:.

   ဘိနပ် အမည်းက အလှဆုံးပဲ။

   Black shoes are the prettiest.

2. A: be-zə-ga: po-hke'-le:, in:-gə-lei'-la: bə-ma-la:?

   ဘယ်စကား ပိုခက်လဲ၊ အင်္ဂလိပ်လား ဗမာလား။

   Which language is more difficult, English or Burmese?

   B: in:-gə-lei'-lo-ga̱ bə-ma-lo-hte' hke'-te.

   အင်္ဂလိပ်လိုက ဗမာလိုထက် ခက်တယ်။

   English is more difficult than Burmese.

   C: in:-gə-lei'-lo-ga̱ bə-ma-lo-hte' mə-hke'-hpu:.

   အင်္ဂလိပ်လိုက ဗမာလိုထက် မခက်ဘူး။

   English is not more difficult than Burmese.

   D: bə-ma-zə-ga: po-hke'-te.

   ဗမာစကား ပိုခက်တယ်။

   Burmese is more difficult.

E: bə-ma-lo ə-hke'-hson:-be.

ဗမာလို အခက်ဆုံးဘဲ။

Burmese is the most difficult.

3.   A: be-o'-hto' po-jai'-thə-le:?

ဘယ်ဦးထုပ် ပိုကြိုက်သလဲ။

Which hat do you like more?

B: di o'-hto' po-jai'-te.

ဒီ ဦးထုပ် ပိုကြိုက်တယ်။

I like this hat more.

4.   A: be-baun:-bi po-nyi'-pa'-thə-le:?

ဘယ်ဘောင်းဘီ ပိုညစ်ပတ်သလဲ။

Which pair of pants are dirtier?

B: ho baun:-bi po-nyi'-pa'-te.

ဟို ဘောင်းဘီ ပိုညစ်ပတ်တယ်။

Those pants are dirtier.

5.   A: se'-ku be-hnə-ywe' shị-le:?

စက္ကူ ဘယ်နှစ်ရွက် ရှိလဲ။

How many sheets of paper do you have?

B: lei:-ywe' shị-de.

လေးရွက် ရှိတယ်။

I have four sheets of paper.

6. A: thu sa-mu-hsa be-hnə-bwe: sa:-le:?
သူ စမူဆာ ဘယ်နှစ်ပွဲ စားလဲ။
How many plates of samosa did he eat?

B: hnə-bwe: sa:-de.
နှစ်ပွဲ စားတယ်။
[He] ate two servings.

7. jə-nọ-hma thon:-hta' ein tə-lon: shi̩-de.
ကျွန်တော့်မှာ သုံးထပ် အိမ် တစ်လုံး ရှိတယ်။
I have a three-story house.

8. A. ko-sein ə-lei:-chein be-lau'-le:?
ကိုစိန် အလေးချိန် ဘယ်လောက်လဲ။
How much does Ko Sein weigh?

B. ko-sein paun tə-ya thon:-ze lei:-de.
ကိုစိန် ကီလို တစ်ရာသုံးဆယ် လေးတယ်။
Ko Sein weighs one hundred-thirty pounds.

9. jə-nɔ myan-ma-pye-go hnə-hka yau'-hpu:-de.
ကျွန်တော် မြန်မာပြည်ကို နှစ်ခါ ရောက်ဖူးတယ်။
I have been to Myanmar two times.

10 A: hsei: be-hnə-lon: thau'-le:?
ဆေး ဘယ်နှစ်လုံး သောက်လဲ။
How many pills did you take?

B: thon:-lon: thau'-te.
     သုံးလုံး သောက်တယ်။
     I took three pills.

11.   thu-hma mei'-hswei ə-mya-ji: shi̤-de.
      သူမှာ မိတ်ဆွေ အများကြီး ရှိတယ်။
      She has a lot of friends.

12.   jə-nɔ-hma sa-o' ə-mya:-ji: shi̤-de.
      ကျွန်တော်မှာ စာအုပ် အများကြီး ရှိတယ်။
      I have the most books.

13. A: be-dain:-pye ə-pu-zon:-le:?
          ဘယ်တိုင်းပြည် အပူဆုံးလဲ။
          Which country is the hottest?

     B: myan-ma-pye-gə̣ ə-pu-zon:-be:.
          မြန်မာပြည်က အပူဆုံးပဲ။
          Myanmar is the hottest.

14. A: di-hpə-na'-nẹ ho-hpə-na' ə-tu-du-be:-la:?
          ဒီဖိနပ်နဲ့ ဟိုဖိနပ် အတူတူပဲလား။
          Are these shoes the same as those shoes?

     B: a-tu-du-be:.
          အတူတူပဲ။
          [They are] the same.

C: mə-tu-bu:.

မတူဘူး။

They are not the same.

15.   di-in:-ji-nẹ ho-in:-ji a-tu-du-be:.

ဒီအကျႌနဲ့ ဟိုအကျႌ အတူတူပဲ။

This shirt and that shirt are the same.

16.   nyaun-shwe-gạ yan-gon-hte' ei:-de.

ညောင်ရွှေက ရန်ကုန်ထက် အေးတယ်။

Nyangshwe is cooler than Yangon.

17.   chaun:-dha-gạ ngạ-pạ-li-hte' mə-wei:-bu:.

ချောင်းသာက ပလီထက် မဝေးဘူး။

Chaungtha is not farther than Ngapali.

18. A: ba'-sa'-ka:-nẹ thwa:-me. ba'-sa'-ka:-gạ yə-hta:-hte'
        myan-de.
        ဘတ်စ်ကားနဲ့ သွားမယ်။ ဘတ်စ်ကားက ရထားထက်
        မြန်တယ်။
        I'll go by bus. The bus is faster than the train.

B: lei-yin-gạ ə-myan-zon:-be:.

လေယာဉ်က အမြန်ဆုံးပဲ။

The plane is the fastest.

Drills

1. Translate the following sentences into Burmese.

I have two glasses of water.

_____

My bag is lighter than your bag.

_____

Bhamo is colder than Mandalay.

_____

2. Do one of the following.

Say in Burmese: "Which tastes better, coffee or tea?" You must say which one tastes better and give at least two reasons why using the word "more".

Say in Burmese what you had (or will have) for all your meals today. You must give the food, drink, and amount of servings. Classifiers must be used.

3. Use the following words to form ten sentences with classifiers.

so စို	hso: ဆိုး	pyin: ပျင်း
se'-bein: စက်ဘီး	ein အိမ်	ə-lei:-chein အလေးချိန်
tau' တောက်	htu ထူ	hmaun မှောင်
pu-de ပူတယ်	wạ-de ဝတယ်	pein-de ပိန်တယ်
to တို	shi-de ရှိတယ်	yei ရေ
lei: လေး	zə-bwe: စားပွဲ	zun: ဇွန်း
nga: ငါး	chan: ချမ်း	chan:-dha ချမ်းသာ
nyi'-pa' ညစ်ပတ်	thon:-ze သုံးဆတယ်	tu တူ
hsin:-ye: ဆင်းရဲ	sa:-de စားတယ်	ei:-de အေးတယ်

Test 9

Match the English words with the Myanmar words.

___	1. strong	a. pya: ပြား
___	2. lazy	b. chau' ချောက်
___	3. poor	c. pyin: ပျင်း
___	4. tall	d. than သန့်
___	5. bicycle	e. hsin:-ye: ဆင်းရဲ
___	6. dark	f. pu ပူ
___	7. flat	g. lei: လေး
___	8. hot	h. se'-bin: စက်ဘီး
___	9. wet	i. myin မြင့်
___	10. heavy	j. hmaun မှောင်
		k. so စို

Match the Myanmar words with their appropriate classifier.

___	1. cups	a. pwe:/bwe: ပွဲ
___	2. letters	b. hte ထည်
___	3. servings	c. saun စောင်
___	4. sheets of paper	d. lon: လုံး
___	5. dogs	e. zi: စီး
___	6. cars	f. hku ခု
___	7. people	g. ywe' ရွက်
___	8. fruit	h. kaun ကောင်
___	9. plastic bottles	i. yau' ယောက်
___	10. horses	j. hkwe' ခွက်
		k. bu: ဘူး

Reading & Writing

Irregularly Pronounced Words

In this section, we will discuss a few other irregular pronunciation
patterns as well as the use of rare consonants and vowels. One
source of irregular patterns is that Pali-derived words often use an
older spelling that has been conserved but no longer conforms to
modern Burmese pronunciation.

သ pronounced as ဖ

Sometimes words that begin with bạ-gon: (သ) are pronounced as
if written with the letter hpạ-o:-hto' (ဖ). The most common
example of this is with the particle hpu/bu which is usually voiced,
but is pronounced as 'hpu'' when it follows a glottal stop as in the
negation of the verb for "like":

don't like	mə-jai'-hpu:	မကြိုက်ဘူး
The city of Pa-an	hpa-an	ဘားအံ

Here are some Pali words used in Buddhism that show this pattern:

monk	hpon:-ji:	ဘုန်းကြီး
monastery	hpon:-ji:-jaun:	ဘုန်းကြီးကျောင်း
pagoda or temple	hpə-ya:	ဘုရား
home altar	hpə-ya:-zin	ဘုရားစင်

Voiced Initial Consonants

Another irregular pattern is to voice a word's initial consonant. This is common with place names and many Burmese towns are so pronounced.

စ pronounced as ဇ

table	zə-bwe:	စားပွဲ
language	zə-ga:	စကား
lemon grass	zə-bə-lin	စပါးလင်
shrine	zei-di	စေတီ
jasmine	zə-be	စံပယ်

ပ pronounced as ဘ

Pagan/Bagan	bə-gan	ပုဂံ
Pegu/Bago	bə-go:	ပဲခူး
beads (used in Buddhist rosaries)	bə-di:	ပတီး

တ or ထ pronounced as ဒ

bridge	də-ta:	တံတား
door	də-ga:	တံခါး
Tavoy/Dawei	də-wei	ထားဝယ်

Words with lạ-tha လ်

Another spelling pattern that comes from Pali, is the inclusion of a şilent lạ-tha' (လ်). Here are a few examples:

university	te'-kə-tho	တက္ကသိုလ်
lieutenant	bo	ဗိုလ်
short haircut, crew cut	bo-kei	ဗိုလ်ကေ
religious merit (cf. kudos)	ku-dho	ကုသိုလ်

Rarely Used Burmese Consonants and Vowels

Eight of the consonants in Burmese are uncommon to rare. The three shown below are found in a few everyday words.

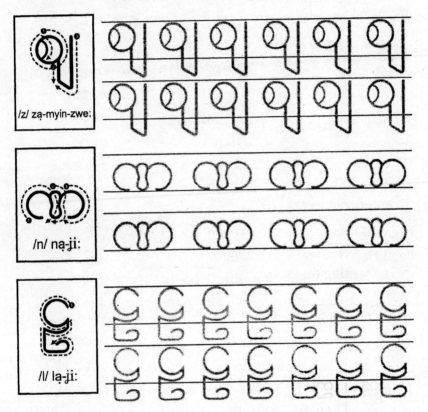

Examples of the use of these letters include the following words:

market	zei:	ဈေး
cheap	zei:-cho-de	ဈေးချိုတယ်
expensive	zei:-ji:-de	ဈေးကြီးတယ်
bank	ban-dai'	ဘဏ်တိုက်
crab	gə-nan:	ဂဏန်း
universe	se'-ja-wə-la	စကြဝဠာ
Garuda	gə-lon	ဂဠုန်

The following five consonants, though still found in the alphabet are rare in modern Burmese. Except for ga-ji:, all are from the third row in alphabet chart.

ဃ	ဋ	ဌ	ဎ	ဎ
/g/	/t/	/ht/	/d/	/d/
ga-ji:	ta̱-tə-lin:-jei	hta̱-wun:-be:	da̱-yin-gau'	da̱-yei-hmo'

Rarely Used Vowels

In reading Burmese, you will occassionally come across words written using special vowel symbols derived from Pali. The following table lists these symbols, along with the more standard form of writing the same vowel using the letter အ.

1	2	3	4	5	6	7
/i̱/	/i/	/u̱/	/u/	/ei/	/ɔ:/	/ɔ/
ဤ	ဤ	ဥ	ဦ	ဧ	ဩ	ဩ်
အိ	အီ	အု	အူ	အေ	အော	အော်

Some examples of words that use these symbols are listed below. When using a dictionary, note that words beginning with these characters are included in the section for the letter အ and in the order shown in the vowel table above.

၏	e'-hkə-ya-ei	/ei/
ဧရာဝတီ	ei-ya-wạ-di	Irrawaddy
ဧပြီ	ei-pi	April
ဧက	ei-kạ	acre

သြ	e'-hkə-ya-ɔ	/ɔ:/
သြဂုတ်	ɔ:-go'	August
သြဇာသီး	ɔ:-za-dhi:	custard apple

| ဉ | e'-hkə-ya-ụ | /ụ/ |
| ဉ | ụ | egg |

| ဦ | e'-hkə-ya-u | /u/ |
| ဦး | u: | uncle, Mr. |

Lesson 10

vocabulary for feelings, family, occupations, animals; subordinate clauses; irregular negative forms; the ၁ prefix and ဝည် suffix; literary form

thin-gan:-za tə-hse: သင်ခန်းစာ ၁၀   Lesson 10
wɔ:-ha-rạ   ဝေါဟာရ   Vocabulary

Nouns

lu-lu'	လူလွတ်	single (unmarried)
lu-pyo	လူပျို	single man
ə-pyo	အပျို	single woman
yi:-za:	ရည်းစား	steady girlfriend/boyfriend, lover
ko-dain	ကိုယ်တိုင်	in person, oneself
ko-bain	ကိုယ်ပိုင်	one's own
tə-yau'-hte:	တစ်ယောက်တည်း	by oneself
ə-mya:-zu	အများစု	mostly, majority
nei-ya	နေရာ	place
ə-hkụ	အခု	now
o'-sa	ဥစ္စာ	property, possession
ə-yei'	အရိပ်	shade
ə-pyen-hma	အပြင်မှာ	outside
də-ga:	တံခါး	door
mi:	မီး	light, fire, electricity
bə-din:-bau'	ပြတင်းပေါက်	window

Verbs

mɔ:-de	မောတယ်	to feel tired
ei'-chin-de	အိပ်ချင်တယ်	to be sleepy
ein-daun jạ-de	အိမ်ထောင် ကျတယ်	to get married
ein-daun-jạ-bi.	အိမ်ထောင် ကျပြီ॥	"[He/She] got married".

hpyi'-te	ဖြစ်တယ်	to be, become
pyɔ-de	ပျော်တယ်	to be happy
wun:-ne:-de	ဝမ်းနည်းတယ်	to be sad, troubled
sho'-te	ရှုပ်တယ်	to be confused
yu:-de	ရူးတယ်	to be crazy
ye'-se'-te	ရက်စက်တယ်	to be cruel
ə-yei:-ji:-de	အရေးကြီးတယ်	to be important
hko'-te.	ခုတ်တယ်	to cut with a machete
aun-de	အောင်တယ်	to pass [a test]
ja-de	ကျတယ်	to fail [a test]
hkin-de	ခင်တယ်	to like someone, be friends
ə-hsin-pyei-de	အဆင်ပြေတယ်	to get along well with someone

Adverbs

-tain:/dain:	တိုင်း	every
nei-dain:	နေ့တိုင်း	daily
la-dain:	လတိုင်း	monthly
hni'-tain:	နှစ်တိုင်း	yearly
mi-dha:-zu	မိသားစု	Family
ə-hpei	အဖေ	father
ə-mei	အမေ	mother
yau'-ja:	ယောက်ျား	husband
mə-ya:, zə-ni:	မယား၊ ဇနီး	wife
ə-go	အကို	older brother
ə-ma	အမ	older sister

maun	မောင်	younger brother of a woman
nyi	ညီ	younger brother of a man
nyi-ma.	ညီမ	younger sister
kə-lei:	ကလေး	child
myei:	မြေး	grandchild
tha:	သား	son
thə-mi:	သမီး	daughter
u:-lei:	ဦးလေး	uncle
ə-dɔ, dɔ-lei:	အဒေါ် ဒေါ်လေး	aunt
ə-hpo:	အဘိုး	grandfather
ə-hpwa:	အဘွား	grandmother
tu	တူ	nephew
tu-ma.	တူမ	niece
yau'-hkə-ma. ə-hpei	ယောက္ခမ အဖေ	father-in-law
yau'-hkə-ma. ə-mei	ယောက္ခမ အမေ	mother-in-law

| ə-lo'-ə-kain | အလုပ်အကိုင် | Occupations |

jaun:-dha:	ကျောင်းသား	student (m)
jaun:-dhu	ကျောင်းသူ	student (f)
hsə-ya	ဆရာ	teacher (m)
hsə-ya-ma.	ဆရာမ	teacher (f)
hsə-ya-wun	ဆရာဝန်	doctor
thwa:-hsə-ya-wun	သွားဆရာဝန်	dentist
shei.-nei	ရှေ့နေ	lawyer
si:-bwa:-yei:-dhə-ma:	စီးပွားရေးသမး	businessperson
kon-dhe	ကုန်သည်	trader

hsain-shin	ဆိုင်ရှင်	shopkeeper, owner
ə-lo'-shin	အလုပ်ရှင်	boss, employer
taun-dhu	တောင်သူ	farmer
le-dhə-ma:	လယ်သမား	rice farmer
tə-nga	တံငါ	fisherman
le'-thə-ma:	လက်သမား	carpenter
se'-pyin	စက်ပြင်	mechanic
a'-cho'-thə-ma:	အပ်ချုပ်သမား	tailor, seamstress
sai'-ka:-dhə-ma:	ဆိုက်ကားသမား	"sidecar" pedaller
bei-din-hsə-ya	ဗေဒင်ဆရာ	fortune teller
sə-yei:	စာရေး	secretary, clerk
zə-bwe:-do:	စားပွဲထိုး	waiter
mə-nei-ja	မန်နေဂျာ	manager
tə-ya:-gan	တရားခံ	criminal
ye:	ရဲ	police officer
thə-mə-dạ	သမ္မတ	president
wun-ji:	ဝန်ကြီး	minister
min:-dha:	မင်းသား	prince (or movie star)
min:-dhə-mi:	မင်းသမီး	princess (or movie star)
yo'-shin-thə-yo'-hsaun	ရုပ်ရှင်သရုပ်ဆောင်	movie actor
si'-tha:	စစ်သား	soldier
si'-bo	စစ်ဗိုလ်	army officer
bo-jo'	ဗိုလ်ချုပ်	general (in army)
sa-yei:-hsə-ya	စာရေးဆရာ	writer

tə-rei'-hsan	တိရစ္ဆာန်	Animals
-hti:	ထီး	male suffix
-mạ	မ	female suffix
hkwei:	ခွေး	dog
jaun	ကြောင်	cat
nga:	ငါး	fish
hnge'	ငှက်	bird
chin-dheị	ခြင်္သေ့	lion
ja:	ကျား	tiger
we'-wun	ဝက်ဝံ	bear
hsin	ဆင်	elephant
kə-la:-o'	ကုလားအုပ်	camel
je'	ကြက်	chicken
be:	ဘဲ	duck
nwa:	နွား	cow
we'	ဝက်	pig
myin:	မြင်း	horse
myau'	မျောက်	monkey
hsei'	ဆိတ်	goat
tho:	သိုး	sheep
wun-bə-lwei	ဝံပုလွေ	wolf
jwe:	ကျွဲ	water buffalo
tau'-tẹ	တောက်တဲ့	large forest gecko
ein-hmyaun	အိမ်မြှောင်	small gecko found inside buildings
mị-jaun:	မိကျောင်း	crocodile

mwei	မြွေ	snake
chin	ခြင်	mosquito
yin-gaun	ယင်ကောင်	fly

Other Useful Words

myọ	မြို့	city
ywa	ရွာ	village
pyi-ne	ပြည်နယ်	state
tain:	တိုင်း	division (Myanmar political unit)
sa-mei:-bwe:	စာမေးပွဲ	test, exam
thi'-pin	သစ်ပင်	tree
pan:	ပန်း	flower
mye'	မြက်	grass
hsan	ဆန်	uncooked rice
nain-ngan-yei:	နိုင်ငံရေး	politics
si:-bwa:-yei:	စီးပွားရေး	economy, economics
tu:-ri'	တူးရစ်	tourist
ə-jin:-daun	အကျဉ်းထောင်	prison
kei'-sa	ကိစ္စ	matter, activity
mə-gə-zin:	မဂ္ဂဇင်း	magazine
kun-pyu-ta	ကွန်ပျူတာ	computer
rei-di-yo	ရေဒီယို	radio
yei-ge:-thi'-ta	ရေခဲသေတ္တာ	refrigerator, freezer
hti:	ထီး	umbrella

Verbs

hkwe:-wei-de	ခွဲဝေတယ်	to share
sai'-te	စိုက်တယ်	to plant, grow
hman-de	မှန်တယ်	to be correct
pyan-de	ပြင်တယ်	to fix, repair
hpwin-de	ဖွင့်တယ်	to open, turn on
pei'-te	ပိတ်တယ်	to close, turn off, shut
si:-bwa:-ye:-lo'-te	စီးပွားရေးလုပ်တယ်	to do business, make a living
myin-de	မြင်တယ်	to see
hta:-de	ထားတယ်	to place, put
ya'-te	ရပ်တယ်	to stop, stand up
ə-the'-shin-de	အသက်ရှင်တယ်	to be alive
thei-de	သေတယ်	to die
pye:-de	ပြေးတယ်	to run
zə-ga:-pyan-lo'-te	စကားပြန်လုပ်တယ်	to translate, interpret
pyan-pei:-ba	ပြန်ပေးပါ	"please translate [for me]"
hta -de	ထတယ်	to rise, go up
hsin:-de	ဆင်းတယ်	to descend, go down (also to get out from)

thə-da   သဒ္ဒါ   **Grammar**

Irregular negative forms

Exceptions to forming the negative form of a verb often occur
when using compounds of a noun plus a verb or sometimes a
"double verb". In such cases, the initial mə particle is added before
the verb instead of the first part of the compound. For example,
when negating the verb for understand, na:-le (နားလည်, literally
"to go around in the ear"), the mə particle is added after the word
for ear:

"[I] don't understand.   na:-**mə**-le-bu:.   နားမလည်ဘူး။

Negating double verb combinations depends on the pattern of the
verb and must be learned individually. An example of a common
double verb is sa:-kaun:-de ((စားကောင်းတယ်, to taste good). In
this case, the negative mə particle is added after the word for eat:

"[It] doesn't taste good.   sa:-**mə**-kaun:-bu:. စားမကောင်ဘူး။

Below is a list of verbs found in this book that use this form:

Verb		Meaning	Negative Form
nei-kaun:-de	နေကောင်းတယ်	to be well	နေမကောင်းဘူး
lan:-shɔ-de	လမ်းလျှောက်တယ်	to walk	လမ်းမလျှောက်ဘူး
le'-hkan-de	လက်ခံတယ်	to receive	လက်မခံဘူး
bai'-hsa-de	ဗိုက်ဆာတယ်	to be hungry	ဗိုက်မဆာဘူး
gaun:- shɔ-de	ခေါင်းလျှော်တယ်	to wash hair	ခေါင်းမလျှော်ဘူး
gaun:-hpi:-de	ခေါင်းဖြီးတယ်	to comb hair	ခေါင်းမဖြီးဘူး
thwa:-tai'-te	သွားတိုက်တယ်	to brush teeth	သွားမတိုက်ဘူး
ei'-ya-dạ-de	အိပ်ရာထတယ်	to get up	အိပ်ရာမထဘူး
ə-lo'-lo'-te	အလုပ်လုပ်တယ်	to work	အလုပ်မလုပ်ဘူး
ə-ei:-mị-de	အအေးမိတယ်	to have a cold	အအေးမမိဘူး
ə-chein-ja-de	အချိန်ကြာတယ်	to take a long time	အချိန်မကြာဘူး
ə-yei:-ji:-de	အရေးကြီးတယ်	to be important	အရေးမကြီးဘူး

Conversation

Ko Min   mi̱-dha:-zṵ be-hne'-yau' shi̱-le:?
ကိုမင်   မိသားစု ဘယ်နှစ်ယောက် ရှိလဲ॥
         How many people are in your family?

John   thon:-yau' shi̱-de. jə-nɔ-ye, jə-nɔ-ye zə-ni:-nḛ tha:.
ဂျွန်   သုံးယောက် ရှိတယ်॥ ကျွန်တော်ရယ် ကျွန်တော်ရဲ့
         ဇနီးနဲ့ သား॥
         There are three people. Myself, my wife and son.

Ko Min   thə-mi: mə-shi̱-bu:-la:?
ကိုမင်   သမီး မရှိဘူးလား॥
         Don't you have any daughters?

John   mə-shi̱-bu:. maun-hnə-ma be-hnə'-yau' shi̱-le:?
ဂျွန်   မရှိဘူး॥ မောင်နှမ ဘယ်နှစ်ယောက် ရှိလဲ॥
         [No, I] don't. How many brothers and sisters
         do you have?

Ko Min   thon:-yau' shi̱-de. ə-go hnə'-yau', nyi-ma tə-yau'.
ကိုမင်   သုံးယောက် ရှိတယ်॥ အကို နှစ်ယောက်၊ ညီမ
         တစ်ယောက်॥
         I have three [brothers and sisters]. [I have] two
         older brothers [and] one younger sister.

wa-ja̱-mya: ဝါကျများ   **Sentences**

1.   A: ein-daun ja̱-bi-la:?
          အိမ်ထောင် ကျပြီလား။
          Is [he] married yet?

     B: ein-daun mə-ja̱-bu:.
          အိမ်ထောင် မကျဘူး။
          [He's] not married.

     C: ein-daun ja̱-pi:-bi.
          အိမ်ထောင် ကျပြီးပြီ။
          [He's] already married.

     D: lu pyu-be:.
          လူ ပျိုပဲ။
          [He's] still single.

2.   A: ba-hpyi'-lo̱ ə-lo'-mə-lo'-le:?
          ဘာဖြစ်လို့ အလုပ်မလုပ်လဲ။
          Why aren't you working?

     B: jə-nɔ mɔ:-lo̱.
          ကျွန်တော် မောလို့။
          Because I'm tired.

     C: jə-ma̱ thei' ei'-chin-lo̱.
          ကျွန်မ သိပ် အိပ်ချင်လို့။
          Because I'm so sleepy.

D: thwa:-sə-ya-mya:-lọ.
    သွားစရာများလို့။
    Because [I have] a lot of errands.

3. A: maun-hnə-mạ be-hnə-yau' shị-le:?
        မောင်နှမ ဘယ်နှစ်ယောက် ရှိလဲ။
        How many brothers and sisters [do you] have?

    B: ə-go tə-yau'-nẹ nyi-mạ tə-yau' shị-de.
        အကို တစ်ယောက်နဲ့ ညီမ တစ်ယောက် ရှိတယ်။
        An older brother [and] a younger sister.

    C: maun-hnə-mạ mə-shị-bu:.
        မောင်နှမ မရှိဘူး။
        [I] don't have [any] brothers or sisters.

4. A: yau'-hkə-mạ-go hkin-la:?
        ယောက္ခမကို ခင်လား။
        Are you friends with your mother-in-law?

    B: ə-hsein mə-pyei-bu:.
        အဆင် မပြေဘူး။
        [I] don't get along [with my mother-in-law].

    C: ho'-kẹ, hkin-de.
        ဟုတ်ကဲ့၊ ခင်တယ်။
        Yes, [I] like [my mother-in-law].

5. A: ba ə-lo' lo'-chin-dhə-le:?
        ဘာ အလုပ် လုပ်ချင်သလဲ။
        What kind of work do [you] want to do?

B: hsə-ya-wun hpyi'-chin-de.
ဆရာဝန် ဖြစ်ချင်တယ်။
[I] want to be a doctor.

C: yo'-shin min:-dhə-mi: hpyi'-chin-de.
ရုပ်ရှင် မင်းသမီး ဖြစ်ချင်တယ်။
[I] want to be a movie princess.

D: le'-thə-ma: hpyi'-chin-de.
လက်သမား ဖြစ်ချင်တယ်။
[I] want to be a carpenter.

A: thu ba-lo'-le:?
သူ ဘာလုပ်လဲ။
What does he do?

B: ko-bain sa:-thau'-hsain hpwiṇ-de.
ကိုယ်ပိုင် စားသောက်ဆိုင် ဖွင့်တယ်။
He opened his own restaurant.

C: le-dhə-ma:.
လယ်သမား။
[He is] a rice farmer.

A: myan-ma-pye-hma ba tə-rei'-hsan-dwei shi̥-le:?
မြန်မာပြည်မှာ ဘာ တိရစ္ဆာန်တွေ ရှိလဲ။
What kind of animals are in Myanmar?

B: myan-ma-pye-hma ja:-dwei ə-mya:-ji: shi̥-de.
မြန်မာပြည်မှာ ကျားတွေ အများကြီး ရှိတယ်။
There are a lot of tigers in Myanmar.

C: myan-ma-pye-hma kə-la:-o' mə-shi̱-bu:.
       မြန်မာပြည်မှာ ကုလားအုပ် မရှိဘူး။
       There are no camels in Myanmar.

8.   pan:-dhi: yei-ge:-thi'-ta-de: htḛ-pei:-ba?
       ပန်းသီး ရေခဲသေတ္တာထဲ ထည့်ပေးပါ။
       Could you put the apples in the refrigerator for me?

9.   thi'-pin-yei'-hma htain-da pyɔ-de.
       သစ်ပင်ရိပ်မှာ ထိုင်တာ ပျော်တယ်။
       [I] enjoy sitting in the shade of the trees.

10. A: sa-mei:-bwe: aun-dhə-la:?
         စာမေးပွဲ အောင်သလား။
         Did [you] pass the test?

     B: aun-de.
         အောင်တယ်။
         [I] passed.

     C: mə-aun-bu:.
         မအောင်ဘူး။
         [I] didn't pass.

     D: jạ-de.
         ကျတယ်။
         [I] failed.

11. A: ti-bwi hpwiṇ-pei:-ba.
         တီဗွီ ဖွင့်ပေးပါ။
         Please turn on the television.

B: mi: pei'-pa.
     မီး ပိတ်ပါ။
     Please turn off the lights.

C: bə-din:-bau' hpwiṇ-yạ-mə-la:?
     ပြတင်းပေါက် ဖွင့်ရမလား။
     May [I] open the window?

D: də-ga: pei'-pa.
     တံခါး ပိတ်ပါ။
     Shut the door, please.

12. tə-rei'-hsan-dwei paun-moṇ mə-sa:-bu:.
     တိရစ္ဆာန်တွေ ပေါင်မုန့် မစားဘူး။
     Animals don't eat bread.

13. ein-hma yin-gaun-dwei ə-mya-ji:-be:.
     အိမ်မှာ ယင်ကောင်တွေ အများကြီးပဲ။
     [My] house has so many flies.

14. ə-pyin-hma mye' sai-hta:-de.
     အပြင်မှာ မြက် စိုက်ထားတယ်။
     I planted grass outside.

15. A: thụ ə-bwa: shị-dhei:-la:?
          သူ့ အဘွား ရှိသေးလား။
          Does he still have a grandmother?

     B: mə-shi-tọ-bi.
          မရှိတော့ဘူး။
          [No,] he doesn't.

C: thụ ə-bwa: shị-de. yan-gon-hma nei-de.

သူ့ အဘွား ရှိတယ်။ ရန်ကုန်မှာ နေတယ်။

He has a grandmother. She lives in Yangon.

16. A: hsə-ya-wun-hsi be-dhu-nẹ thwa:-le:?

ဆရာဝန်ဆီ ဘယ်သူနဲ့ သွားလဲ။

Who did you go to the doctor with?

B: hsə-ya-wun-hsi tə-yau'-hte: thwa:-de.

ဆရာဝန်ဆီ တစ်ယောက်တည်း သွားတယ်။

I went to the doctor by myself.

17. A: be-dhụ-go mye' hko'-hkain:-le:?

ဘယ်သူ့ကို မြက် ခုတ်ခိုင်းလဲ။

Who did [he] ask to cut the grass?

B: thụ-ko-dain hko'-te.

သူ့ကိုယ်တိုင် ခုတ်တယ်။

[He] cut [the grass] by himself.

18. ko-dain ba-dha-pyan-de.

ကိုယ်တိုင် ဘာသာပြန်တယ်။

I translated it by myself.

19. jə-mạ yau'-ja: ko-dain zə-bin hnya'-te.

ကျွန်မ ယောက်ျား ကိုယ်တိုင် ဆံပင် ညှပ်တယ်။

My husband cuts his own hair.

20. myan-ma-za tə-yau'-hte: thin-da pyɔ-de.

မြန်မာစာ တစ်ယောက်တည်း သင်တာ ပျော်တယ်။

I enjoy studying Myanmar by myself.

21. A: da be-dhu̯ ha-le:?

ဒါ ဘယ်သူ့ ဟာလဲ။

Whose is this?

B: jə-nɔ̰ o'-sa.

ကျွန်တော့ ဥစ္စာ။

[This is] mine.

22.   thu̯ in:-ji ə-yan: hla̰-de.

သူ့ အကျႍိ အရမ်း လှတယ်။

Her blouse is very pretty.

23. A: da be-dhu̯ le'-kau'-le:?

ဒါ ဘယ်သူ့ လက်ကောက်လဲ။

Whose bracelet is this?

B: e:-da jə-ma̰-yḛ le'-kau'.

အဲဒါ ကျွန်မရဲ့ လက်ကောက်။

That is my bracelet.

C: be-dhu̯ o'-sa-le: mə-thḭ-bu:.

ဘယ်သူ့ ဥစ္စာလည်း မသိဘူး။

[I] don't know whose this is.

D: da thu̯ o'-sa, jə-nɔ̰ o'-sa mə-ho'-hpu:.

ဒါ သူ့ ဥစ္စာ၊ ကျွန်တော့ ဥစ္စာ မဟုတ်ဘူး။

It's hers, not mine.

Drills

1. Translate the following sentences into Myanmar.

   My girlfriend went home.

   She has three younger sisters.

   What movie star do you like most?

2. Do the following.

   Describe your family in Burmese. You must tell how many family members you have and identify each member.

   Tell what occupation you would like to do (or currently do) and give at least one reason why.

3. Use the following words to form ten sentences.

yi:-za: ရည်းစား	mɔ:-de မောတယ်	yu: ရှူး
lạ-dain: လတိုင်း	ə-hkụ အခု	ein-daun အိမ်ထောင်
tain: တိုင်း	nei-ya နေရာ	hpwiṇ-de ဖွင့်တယ်
hpon:-ji: ဘုန်းကြီး	pyɔ ပျော်	ə-yei:-ji: အရေးကြီး
kə-lei: ကလေး	tha: သား	thə-mi: သမီး
hkwei: ခွေး	we' ဝက်	hsə-ya-wun ဆရာဝန်
mwei မြွေ	yin ယင်	zə-bwe:-do: စားပွဲထိုး
si'-tha: စစ်သား	hsin ဆင်	le'-thə-ma: လက်သမား
jaun ကြောင်	chin ခြင်	mi: မီး
-hti: ထီး	pan: ပန်း	ə-lo'-ə-kain အလုပ်အကိုင်
ywa ရွာ	mɔ:-de မောတယ်	sai'-te စိုက်တယ်

Test 10

Match the English words with the Myanmar words.

_____ 1. mother		a. hman-de မှန်တယ်
_____ 2. to be confusing		b. on:-dhi အုန်းသီး
_____ 3. tree		c. myin-de မြင်တယ်
_____ 4. village		d. yə-hta: ရထား
_____ 5. coconut		e. chin ခြင်
_____ 6. to see		f. ei'-chin-de အိပ်ချင်တယ်
_____ 7. pig		g. nei-de နေတယ်
_____ 8. to sit		h. sho'-te ရှုပ်တယ်
_____ 9. to live		i. rei-di-yo ရေဒီယို
_____ 10. husband		j. ywa ရွာ
_____ 11. to be crazy		k. thi'-pin သစ်ပင်
_____ 12. sleepy		l. htain-de ထိုင်တယ်
_____ 13. to be correct		m. yau'-ja ယောက်ျား
_____ 14. waiter		n. hsə-ya-wun ဆရာဝန်
_____ 15. doctor		o. yu:-de ရူးတယ်
		p. ə-mei အမေ
		q. zə-bwe:-do: စားပွဲထိုး
		r. we' ဝက်

Write the appropriate form of address to use when speaking to the people below:

1. A woman who is much older than you   _____

2. A man who is much older than you   _____

3. A woman five years younger than you   _____

4. A five year old boy   _____

5. A stranger who is about your age   _____

6. A monk   _____

7. Your boss (a man)   _____

8. A close friend   _____

9. A novice monk   _____

10. Your doctor   _____

11. A man five years older than you   _____

12. Your teacher (a lady)   _____

Reading & Writing

Literary Form

Nearly every language shows some divergence between spoken and literary styles and Burmese is no exception. In fact, the literary and spoken forms are more different than in English. The main way that Burmese literary form differs from spoken form is in the particles that each form uses. For example, the particles attached to nouns for "to" and "for" are different in literary and spoken form. Literary form also has special particles to indicate the present/past and future verb forms. In addition, literary form sometimes uses special abbreviations.

Literary form in Burmese is also used in many everyday situations including dictionaries, signs and restaurant menus. Thus, it is useful for even an introductory student of Burmese to be able to recognize the literary form of Burmese. This brief introduction to literary form of Burmese will enable you to identify and understand some very common examples of literary form.

For example, a sign saying "to the bathroom" would be written:

အိမ်သာသို့ (ein-da-dhọ)   instead of   အိမ်သာကို (ein-da-ko)

or the dictionary entry for "to go" might be written like this:

သွားသည် (thwa:-thi)   instead of   သွားတယ် (thwa:-de)

Literary Abbreviations

The Burmese literary form also contains some special characters
which are used in place of the more easily recognized spelling
using letters from the Burmese alphabet.

Symbol	Name	Sound	Primary Function or Meaning
၏	e'-hkə-ya-i̯	/i̯/	possessive form = ရဲ့
၍	e'-hkə-ya-i	/i/	this = ဒီ
၌	e'-hkə-ya-yue	/yue/	so, because = လို့
၎	e'-hkə-ya-hnai'	/hnai'/	at, in, on = မှာ

Spoken and Written Forms Compared

Spoken	Written	Function or Meaning
Particles		
တယ် (-te)	သည် (-thi)	present/past sentence particle
မယ် (-me)	မည် (-mi)	future sentence particle
ကို (-ko)	သို့ (-tho̯)	to place or time
က (-ka̯)	မှ (-hma̯)	from place or time
မှာ (-hma)	၌ (-hnai')	at, in, on
ရဲ့ (-ye̯)	၏ (-i̯)	possessive form
သလဲ: (-thə-le:)	သနည်း (-thə-ne:)	question
ရင် (-yin)	လျှင် (hlin)	if, when
လို့ (-lo̯)	၍ (-ywei̯)	so, because
လဲ (-le:)	လည်း (-le:)	also, as well
လဲ (-le:)	နည်း (-ni:)	question marker

နဲ့ (-ne̠)   နှင့် (-niṇ)   and
မ..ဘူး (-mə...bu:) မ (-ma̠)   not
ဖို့ (-hpọ)   ရန်(-yan)   in order to
လောက် (-lau') ခန့် (-hkan)   about

Nouns and Verbs

နင်(nin); မင်း(min)	သင် (-thin)	you
နာမည် (-na-me)	အမည် (-i)	name
အခု (ə-kụ)	ယခု(yə-kụ)	now
ဘယ်သူ (be-dhu)	မည်သူ(mi-dhu)	who
ဒီ (di)	ဤ(i)	this
အဲ့ဒီ (e:-di),ဟို(ho)	ထို(hto)	that
ဒီ(di)	သည်(thi)	this
ပဲ (-pe)	ပင်(-pin)	emphatic
no spoken form	ဖြစ် (-hpyi')	to be

Reading Exercise

Read the following aloud and translate into English.

A.

၁   မင်္ဂလာပါ ဆရာ။

၂   နေကောင်းရဲ့လား။

၃   နာမည် ဘယ်လိုခေါ်လဲ။

၄   ရပါတယ်။

၅   နားမလည်ဘူး။

၆   ကျွန်မ မြန်မာလူမျိုးပါ။

၇   ဒါ ဘယ်လောက်လဲ။

၈   ကျွန် အမေရိကန် လူမျိုးပါ။

၉   အိမ်သာ ဘယ်မှာလဲ။

၁၀   အိမ်သာ ညာဘက်မှာ။

၁၁   စာအုပ် ကုလားထိုင်အောက်မှာ။

၁၂   ဒီ ပန်း သိပ်လှတယ်။

၁၃   ဒီနေ့ ဘာနေ့လဲ။

၁၄   ဒီနေ့ အင်္ဂါနေ့။

၁၅   မနက်ပိုင်း ကျောင်း သွားတယ်။

၁၆   ကျွန်တော် တရုတ်အစားအစာ သွားစားမယ်။

၁၇   အခု ဘယ်နှစ်နာရီ ရှိသလဲ။

၁၈   ၈:နာရီမှာ လေဆိပ် သွားမယ်။

၁၉   ကိုဇော် ဘုရား သွားတာ ကြိုက်တယ်။

၂၀   ခင်ဗျား ကား ဘာ အရောင် ရှိလဲ။

B.

၁   ဘယ်က ပြန်လာလဲ။

၂   မြန်မာစာ သွားသင်မလို့။

၃   ကျွန်တော် တရုတ်အစားအစာ မကြိုက်ဘူး။

၄   သူ့အိမ်မှာ ခွေး ရှိတယ်။

၅   နောက်လမှာ တရုတ်ပြည် သွားမယ်။

၆   တနလ်ာနေ့ ကျွန်တော် ဒီမှာ မရှိဘူး။

၇   ကျွန်မ အမေရိကမှာ အင်္ဂလိပ်စာ သွားသင်မယ်။

၈   ဂျပန် စားသောက်ဆိုင်မှာ အလုပ်လုပ်ချင်တယ်။

၉   အိမ်သာ အပေါ်ထပ်မှာ။

၁၀   ကျွန်တော် စာအုပ် ရေးနေတယ်။

၁၁   ကျွန်မ အင်္ဂလိပ်စကား နည်းနည်း ပြောတတ်တယ်။

၁၂   ဒီနေ့ အရမ်း မောတယ်။

၁၃   ဒီ စာအုပ် ဘယ်သူ့စာအုပ်လဲ။

၁၄   ဒီနေ့ သိပ် ပူတယ်နော်။

၁၅   ခင်ဗျားရဲ့ ရည်းစား နာမည် ဘယ်လို ခေါ်သလဲ။

၁၆   ကျွန်တော် နေ့တိုင်း ရေချိုးတယ်။

၁၇   ကျွန်မ တနင်္ဂနွေနေ့တိုင်း အဝတ်လျှော်တယ်။

၁၈   ဈေးကြီးလို့ သူ ကား မဝယ်ဘူး။

၁၉   အခု ခေါင်း အရမ်း ကိုက်တယ်။

၂၀   ကျွန်တော် နေ့တိုင်း နှစ်ခါ သွားတိုက်တယ်။

C.

၁ အမေရိကန်က တရုတ်ပြည်ထက် ကြီးတယ်။
၂ အဲဒီ ကား သိပ် ပိုလှတယ်။
၃ သူ့မှာ ခွေး သုံးကောင် ရှိတယ်။
၄ ကျွန်မ အမဲရောင်ကို အနီရောင်ထက် ကြိုက်တယ်။
၅ ကျွန်မ အကို ဘုရား သွားချင်တယ်။
၆ သူ့ အကို ဘာ အလုပ် လုပ်လဲ။
၇ ကချင်ပြည်နယ်မှာ တောင် အမြင့်ဆုံး ရှိတယ်။
၈ မောင်နှမ ဘယ်နှစ်ယောက် ရှိလဲ။
၉ ကျွန်မ အကို နှစ်ယောက် ရှိတယ်။
၁၀ မနေ့က ကျွန်တော် အင်္ကျီ တစ်ထည် ဝယ်တယ်။
၁၁ မစိန် တရုတ်စကား အရမ်း ပြောတတ်တယ်နော်။
၁၂ ခင်ဗျား ဘာဖြစ်လို့ ကျောင်းမသွားလဲ။
၁၃ ဆရာဝန် ဖြစ်ချင်တယ်။
၁၄ ခင်ဗျား အသက် ဘယ်လောက်လဲ။
၁၅ သူ့မှာ ရည်းစား ဘယ်နှစ်ယောက် ရှိလဲ။
၁၆ နေ့တိုင်း လမ်းလျှောက်တယ်။
၁၇ မနက်ဖြန် ဆံပင် သွားညှပ်မယ်။
၁၈ ကျွန်မ အဝတ်စားလဲနေတယ်။
၁၉ မနက်ဖြန် ရုပ်ရှင် သွားကြည့်မယ်။
၂၀ ခင်ဗျား ပိုက်ဆံ အများကြီး ရှိရင် ဘာလုပ်မလဲ။

D.

၁ ဒီနေ့ သိပ် နေမကောင်းဘူး။
၂ မနက်ဖြန် အလည် သွားမယ်။
၃ အင်္ဂလိပ်စကား သင်တာပျော်ဖို့ ကောင်းတယ်။
၄ အကို စာအုပ် ဖတ်တာ သိပ် ကြိုက်တယ်။
၅ ကျွန်မ အဒေါ် မော်လမြိုင်မှာ နေတယ်။
၆ မီးရထား နောက်နာရီဝက်မှာ လာမယ်။
၇ အင်္ဂလိပ် သတင်းစာ ဟိုစားပွဲ ပေါ်မှာ ရှိတယ်။
၈ စာအုပ်ဆိုင် စာတိုက်ရှေ့မှာ ရှိတယ်။
၉ မြန်မာ မိန်းကလေး နေ့တိုင်း ထဘီ ဝတ်ထားတယ်။
၁၀ ကျွန်တော့် အကို ကား မောင်းတယ်။
၁၁ ဘာဖြစ်လို့ သူ မလိုက်လဲ။
၁၂ ပုစွန်ဟင်း အရမ်း စပ်လို့ စားမရဘူး။
၁၃ ပုဂံမှာ ဘုရားတွေ အများကြီး ရှိတယ်။
၁၄ တရုတ်ပြည်က မြန်မာပြည်ထက် ကြီးတယ်။
၁၅ မနက်ဖြန် ကျွန်တော်နဲ့ လက်ဖက်ရည်ဆိုင်မှာ တွေ့မလား။
၁၆ ဟို လမ်းမှာ အီတလီ စားသောက်ဆိုင် ရှိတယ်။
၁၇ ကျွန်တော့် အကို ပြီးခဲ့တဲ့လမှာ အိမ်ထောင်ကျတယ်။
၁၈ ခင်ဗျားဆီ မနက်ဖြန် ဖုန်းဆက်မယ်။
၁၉ ကချင်ပြည်နယ် မြန်မာပြည်မှာ ရှိတယ်။
၂၀ မြန်မာပြည်မှာ ဧရာဝတီမြစ် အရှည်ဆုံးပဲ။

E.

မနေ့က စနေနေ့၊ အလုပ် မလုပ်ဘူး။ သူငယ်ချင်း
နှစ် ယောက်နဲ့ လက်ဖက်ရည်ဆိုင်မှာ တွေ့တယ်။
လက်ဖက်ရည် သုံးခွက် သောက်တယ်။ ရေ
တစ်ပုလင်း သောက်တယ်။ ဆမူဆာ ငါးခုနဲ့
ပလာတာ လေးခုလည်း စားတယ်။ နောက်ပြီး
ကန်တော်ကြီး ပန်းခြံမှာ လမ်းလျှောက်တယ်။

F.

မိသားစု ငါးယောက် ရှိတယ်။ မော်လမြိုင်မှာ
နေတယ်။ အမေ ဆရာဝန်နဲ့ အဖေ ကျောင်းဆရာ
ဖြစ်တယ်။ အကို တစ်ယောက်နဲ့ ညီမ
တစ်ယောက် ရှိတယ်။ ခွေးလည်း ရှိတယ်။ သူ့
နာမည် အနီ ခေါ်တယ်။

Appendix I

A Brief Overview of Burmese Grammar

Appendix I. An Overview of Burmese Grammar

Burmese grammar is very different from English in several ways. The Subject-Object-Verb sentence structure which places the verb at the end of the sentence is perhaps the more important difference when compared to English. Another major difference is the heavy use of particles which take on a variety of roles. The use of descriptive verbs in the place of adjectives is yet another.

Most Burmese words are monosyllabic, although words coming from Sanskrit or Pali tend to be polysyllabic. Sentences are made up of one or more noun phrases followed by the verb phrase. These phrases are amalgams created by attaching particles, or by combining nouns with other nouns and verbs with other verbs to form noun and verb phrases. In addition to nouns, verbs and particles, one may occasionally see an adverb, which is a fourth category of words, which is included before the verb phrase.

While nouns and verbs can be freestanding, particles are always attached to other words, usually as suffixes. Particles play a critical role in Burmese grammar, taking on a number of functions such as verb endings, conjunctions and prepositions. Particle classes include verb particles, noun particles, question particles and clause-ending particles. A list of the spoken Burmese particles used in this book is presented below.

Fortunately, Burmese speakers tend to use short, simple sentences in ordinary conversation. A verb plus a particle can be a sentence, without a subject or object. Noun phrases are often completely left out and only added for clarity. Also, there is no verb for "to be" so English sentences like "She is a teacher", or "I am Canadian" are said using just the noun or noun phrase without any verb.

Particles Used in This Book

Verb particles

- -te တယ် present/past final particle L2
- -dhə- သ present/past particle used when not in final position L2
- -me မယ် future final particle L3
- -mə- မ future particle used when not in final position L3
- -pi/bi ပြီ past perfect particle (e.g., sa-bi စာပြီ "have/has eaten") L3
- mə.(verb).hpu:/bu: မ... ဘူး creates a negative form of a verb L2
- -hpu:/bu: ဖူး to have ever done L7
- -yạ ရ command form of a verb must L8
- -on: ဦး indicates continuing or further action, L7
- -kẹ/gẹ ခဲ့ indicates movement to or from a person L3

Noun particles

- -hma မှာ at the place of, at the time of L2
- -ko ကို used to indicate movement to a place L4
- -ka က used to indicate movement from a place L4
- -ne နဲ့ and, with, by (to indicate type of transport) L1
- -lau' လောက် about L1
- -ye. ရဲ့ possessive L4
- -le လည်း also sometimes used as v.p. to mean "and" between two verbs L2
- -gɔ: ကော shows emphasis can be translated as "as for..." L1
- -hsi ဆီ used to indicate movement to or from a person L6
- -dwe တွေ plural form L8
- gender forms: L8
- -hte' ထက် more than L9
- -hson: ဆုံး most, best, last L9

Noun forming particles

- a- အ L4
- -da တာ L4

Subordinate clause particles

- -hpọ/bọ ဖို့ in order to L7
- -lọ လို့ because L7
- -yin ရင် if L7

Final sentence particles

- -la: လား final "Yes/ No" question particle L1
- -le: လဲ final question particle L1
- -nɔ? နော် final particle meaning "right" or "isn't it?" L1

General particles (used in both noun and verb phrases)

- -pa ပါ polite particle L1
- be: ဘဲ particle used to indicate emphasis, or "only" L6

Appendix II

Test and Writing Exercise Answers

Appendix II. Test and Writing Exercise Answers

Test 1

Matching

1. e   2. j   3. b   4. f   5. g   6. a   7. d   8. c   9. k   10. i

Translation

1. What is this? This is a watch (polite particle).
2. How are you?
3. Nice to meet you.
4. hsɔ-ri:-nɔ? ဆောရီးနော်။
5. da thə-din:-za-nɔ? ဒါ သတင်းစာနော်။

Test 2

Matching

1. a	2. p	3. o	4. n	5. i
6. m	7. g	8. j	9. d	10. h
11. f	12. r	13. e	14. k	15. q

Translation

1. He/she is studying Burmese.
2. He/she is studying over there.
3. I live in Japan.
4. ein-da be-hma-le:? အိမ်သာ ဘယ်မှာလဲ။
5. mye'-hman zə-bwe:-pɔ-hma shị-de. မျက်မှန် စားပွဲပေါ်မှာ ရှိတယ်။

Test 3

Matching

1. j	2. n	3. e	4. h	5. k	6. o
7. g	8. b	9. m	10. d	11. c	12. f

Translation

1. He/she can write in Myanmar.
2. May I go to the toilet?
3. He/she wants to go to the bookstore.
4. jə-nɔ hkau'-swe:-zain-go thwa:-me. ကျွန်တော် လေဆိပ်ကို သွားမယ်။
5. thu-go yo'-shin-yon-hma shi-de. သူတို့ ရုပ်ရှင်ရုံမှာ ရှိတယ်။

Test 4

Matching

| 1. m | 2. l | 3. f | 4. e | 5. j | 6. q | 7. d |
| 8. o | 9. b | 10. g | 11. c | 12. i | 13. a | 14. k |

Translation

1. How many cars do you have?.
2. I don't want to go to the store. It's too far.
3. If [we] go to the pagoda, how much will it be?
4. di:-te'-kə-si a:-la:? ဒီ တက္ကစီ အားလား။
5. zei:-ji:-de. thon:-dauṇ nga:-ya ja' yạ-mə-la:?
   ဈေးကြီးတယ်။ သုံးထောင့် ငါးရာကျပ် ရမလား။

Word Exercise

1. သိတယ်   2. တတ်တယ်   3. မှတ်မိတယ်
4. တတ်တယ်   5. သိတယ်

Test 5

A. Write these times in Burmese.

1. မနက် လေးနာရီ
2. ည ခြောက်နာရီ
3. သန်းခေါင်
4. ညနေ သုံးနာရီ ငါးဆယ်မိနစ်
5. မနက် ဆယ့်တစ်နာရီခွဲ
6. ည ဆယ်နာရီ လေးဆယ့်ငါးမိနစ်
7. ည ငါးနာရီ ငါးမိနစ်

B. Write these times in English.

1. seven in the evening (7:00 p.m.)
2. three at night (3:00 a.m.)
3. six in the morning (6:00 a.m.)
4. two forty-four in the afternoon (2:45 p.m.)
5. ten twenty-five in the morning (10:25 a.m.)
6. afternoon.
7. four in the evening (4:00 p.m.)

C. Translation

1. I will arrive about three o'clock.
2. I go to work at five in the morning.
3. I want to sleep during the morning.
4. bil-ye jaun: nya-nei lei:-na-yi hsin-de.
   ဘီလ်ရဲ့ ကျောင်း ညနေ လေးနာရီ ဆင်းတယ်။
5. e:-da sa-o' hpa'-pi:-bi. အဲဒါ စာအုပ် ဖတ်ပြီးပြီ။
6. yo'-shin-yon-ko lai'-me-la:? ရုပ်ရှင်ရုံကို လိုက်မလား။

Test 6

Matching: Months

| 1. i | 2. l | 3. h | 4. k | 5. a | 6. j |
| 7. e | 8. c | 9. d | 10. g | 11. f | 12. b |

Days

| 1. c | 2. g | 3. b | 4. a | 5. e | 6. d | 7. f |

Translation

1. I rest from Saturday to Monday..
2. Sometimes I go to sleep at midnight.
3. I will go to Vietnam in November.
4. nau'-hnə-la-hma man:-də-lei:-go thwa:-me.
   နောက်နှစ်လမှာ မန္တလေးကို သွားမယ်။
5. thu chau'-na-yi: kə-de-gạ saụn-nei-de.
   သူ ခြောက်နာရီ ကတည်းက စောင့်နေတယ်။

Test 7

Matching

| 1. f | 2. h | 3. k | 4. n | 5. m | 6. e |
| 7. c | 8. d | 9. j | 10. i | 11. l | 12. g |

Translation

1. I like Myanmar food but I don't like Vietnamese food.
2. Is Ma So So at home?
3. Myanmar curry is not very spicy.
4. di hin:-jo ayan: ngan-de. mə-sa:-nain-bu:.
   ဒီ ဟင်းချို အရမ်း ငန်တယ်။ မစားနိုင်ဘူး။
5. shan:-hkau'-hswe: sa:-bu:-dhə-la:? ရှမ်းခေါက်ဆွဲ စားဖူးသလား။

Test 8

Matching

1. d	2. m	3. b	4. g	5. f	6. l
7. a	8. e	9. k	10. h	11. c	12. j

Translation

1. You can't wear shoes in the pagoda.
2. She is wearing a white blouse and blue pants.
3. I have diarrhea. My head also aches.
4. jə-nɔ ə-wo'-ə-sa: ə-thi' lo-de. ကျွန်တော် အဝတ်အစား အသစ် လိုတယ်။
5. thụ o'-to' ə-yan: ji-de. သူ့ ဦးထုပ် အရမ်း ကြီးတယ်။

Test 9

Matching

1. d	2. c	3. e	4. i	5. h
6. j	7. a	8. f	9. k	10. g

Classifiers

1. j	2. c	3. a	4. g	5. h
6. e	7. i	8. d	9. k	10. e

Test 10

Matching

1. p	2. h	3. k	4. j	5. b
6. c	7. r	8. l	9. g	10. m
11. o	12. f	13. a	14. q	15. n

Forms of Address

1. ဒေါ်   2. ဦး:   3. ညီမ   4. မောင်
5. ရှင် ၊ ခင်ဗျာ: 6. ဦး:ဇင်:   7. ဆရာ ၊ ဦး:လေး: 8. နင် ၊ မင်:
9. ကိုရင်   10. ဆရာ   11. အကို   12. ဆရာမ

Writing Exercise Answers

Writing Exercise 1

1. ကား:   2. ကူး:   3. ခါ:   4. ၃
5. ငါ:   6. စာ:   7. စီ:   8. စကား:
9. ဆာ:   10. ဆီ   11. ဆေး:   12. အာ:

Writing Exercise 2

1. ကိုး:   2. ခေါင်း:   3. ဂီတ   4. စောင်း:
5. စကတ်   6. ဆိုင်   7. ဆိုး:   8. ဇက်
9. ဇစ်   10. ညာ   11. ညီ   12. တစ်
13. တူ   14. ထူ   15. ထိုင်   16. အတူတူ

Writing Exercise 3

1. နိုင်   2. တီဗီ   3. ဖတ်   4. ထမင်:
5. ခေါ်   6. အိမ်   7. အထဲ   8. မေး:
9. နောက်   10. စာတိုက်   11. ကောင်:   12. စာအုပ်
13. ညနေ   14. ခက်   15. မိနစ်   16. ပန်:ခြီ
17. အနီ   18. အထိ

Writing Exercise 4

1. လမ်း　　2. အိမ်သာ　　3. ဒီဟာ　　4. ဝေး

5. အဝါ　　6. ဓာတ်ပုံ　　7. မျက်မှန်　　8. တယ်လီဖုန်း

9. သင်တယ်　　10. လွယ်　　11. ရပါတယ်　　12. နေး

13. ဟိုတယ်　　14. စားသောက်ဆိုင်　　15. လိပ်စာ

16. ဟုတ်ကဲ့　　17. မြန်မာစာ　　18. သွား

Writing Exercise 5

1. ၁၂၃　　2. ၆၇၆　　3. ၅၆၀　　4. ၂၀၈၄

5. ၃၅၆၁　　6. ၁၈၇၃　　7. ၂၄၆၂　　8. ၅၆၃၇

9. အဂီနေ့ မနက်　　10. ပြင်သစ်လူမျိုး

11. ဘက်စ်ကား နံပါတ် ၄၅　　12. ဓာတ်ပုံ ရိုက်မလား။

13. ဒီကို လာပါရင်။　　14. ၂၆၄ ပန်းဆိုးတန်း လမ်း

15. မီးရထား ခြောက်နာရီ ရောက်တယ်။

16. ဒီနေ့ ပန်းခြံ သွားမယ်။

17. အင်္ဂလိပ်စကား ပြောတတ်လား။

18. ဒီ လမ်းမှာ ထိုင်း သံရုံး ရှိတယ်။

Writing Exercise 6

1. nga:-**daun** lei:-ze-ba. ငါးထောင် လေးဆယ်ပါ။

2. te'-kə-tho-go nei̯-gin:-hma thwa:-ji̯n-de. တက္ကသိုလ်ကို
နေ့ခင်းမှာ သွားချင်တယ်။

3. mə-ho'-pu. **bə-go-gạ** mə-la-bu:. မဟုတ်ဘူး။ပဲခူးကမလာဘူး။

4. jei:-zu-tin-ba-de. thwa:-**bi**. ကျေးဇူးတင်ပါတယ်။ သွားပြီ။

5. bə-ma-zə-ga: mə-hke'-hpu. ဗမာစကား မခက်ဘူး။

6. myan-ma-**za** yei:-**da'**-la:? မြန်မာစာ ရေးတတ်တယ်လား။

7. shwe-**da**-gon-hpə-ya: thwa:-pi:-**bi**. ရွှေတိဂုံဘုရား သွားပြီးပြီ။

8. pi:-**gẹ**-**dẹ**-chau'-lạ yan-gon-**go** thwa:-**de**. ပြီးခဲ့တဲ့ခြောက်လ ရန်ကုန်ကို သွားတယ်။

9. twẹi-yạ-da wun:-**dha-ba-de**. တွေ့ရတာ ဝမ်းသာပါတယ်။

10. sa-o' hpa'-chin-**de**. စာအုပ် ဖတ်ချင်တယ်။

Writing Exercise 7

1. tə-htaun **hnə**-ya ja'. တစ်ထောင့် ငါးရာ ကျပ်။

2. thu **thə**-yei kə-lə-htain-hma htain-jin-de. သူ သားရေ ကုလားထိုင်မှာ ထိုင်ချင်တယ်။

3. **zə** -bwe:-do, di-nei **ngə**-man: hin:-jo shi-la:? စားပွဲထိုး၊ ဒီနေ့ ငါးမန်း ဟင်းချို ရှိလား။

4. **bə** -go ba'-sa'-ka:-nẹ **hnə**-na-yi ja-de. ပဲခူးကို ဘတ်စ်ကားနဲ့ နှစ်နာရီ ကြာတယ်။

5. **ngə**-pyɔ-dhi-nẹ **ngə**-pi-yei **zə**-bwe-pɔ-hma. ၄က်ပျောသီးနဲ့ ငါးပိရည် စားပွဲပေါ်မှာ။

6. **bə**-zun-hin: tə -bwe: sa:-jin-de. ပုဇွန်ဟင်း တစ်ပွဲ စားချင်တယ်။

7. ko-htun: mo: **bə**-mo-gạ la:-de. thu ə-the' **hnə**-hse shi-bi. ကိုထွန်း မူး ဝန်းမော်က လာတယ်။ သူ အသက် နှစ်ဆယ် ရှိပြီ။

8. a-nan-da-**pə**-hto: **bə**-gan-hma shi-de. အာနန္ဒာပုထိုး ပုဂံမှာ ရှိတယ်။

Writing Exercise 8

1. thu yan-gon-tə-ka-to-hma thin-nei-de. သူ

ရန်ကုန်တက္ကသိုလ်မှာ သင်နေတယ်။

2. gə-ba-jɔ-la'-hpe'-ye-zain thwa:-me. lai'-mə-la:?

ကမ္ဘာကျော် လက်ဖက်ရည်ဆိုင် သွားမယ်။ လိုက်မလား။

3. kei'-sə-mə-shi̱-ba-bu: ကိစ္စမရှိပါဘူး။

4. mə-ne'-hpyan ta-rei-hsan-yon thwa:-jin-de. မနက်ဖြန်

တိရိစ္ဆာန်ရုံ သွားချင်တယ်။

5. pon-hman mo:-ya-dhi-hma pein-ne:-dhi sa:-de. ပုံမှန် မိုးရာသီမှာ

ပိန္နဲသီး စားတယ်။

6. thu jə-pan kon-bə-ni-hma ə-lo'-lo'-de. သူ ဂျပန် ကုမ္ပဏီမှာ

အလုပ်လုပ်တယ်။

7. nau'-la̱ man-də-lei:-go thwa:-me. နောက်လ မန္တလေးကို

သွားမယ်။

8. ngwei-se'-ku hnə-ya shi-la:? ငွေစက္ကူ နှစ်ရာ ရှိလား။

Appendix III

Useful Words and Phrases

Appendix III. Useful Words and Phrases

General Conversation

How are you?	nei-kaun-yẹ-la?	နေကောင်းရဲ့လား။
Have you eaten yet?	sa:-pi:-bi-la:?	စားပြီးပြီလား။
Where're you going?	be thwa:-mə-le:	ဘယ် သွားမလဲ။
goodbye	thwa:-bi	သွားပြီ
[I'm] fine.	nei-kaun:-ba-de.	နေကောင်းပါတယ်
[I'm] not so well	mə-kaun:-bu:	မကောင်းဘူး
so-so, normal	di-lo-be:	ဒီလိုပဲ။
See you later.	nau'-hma tweị-me.	နောက်မှ တွေ့မယ်။
See you tomorrow.	mə-ne'-hpyan tweị-me.	မနက်ဖြန် တွေ့မယ်။
Please to meet you.	tweị-ya-da	တွေ့ရတာ
	wun:-tha-ba-de	ဝမ်းသာပါတယ်
Thank you.	jei:-zu:-tin-ba-de.	ကျေးဇူး တင်ပါတယ်
I'm sorry.	sɔ-ri:-nɔ?	ဆောရီးနော်
what?	ba-le:	ဘာလဲ
where?	be-hma-le:	ဘယ်မှာလဲ
when?	be-dɔ-le:	ဘယ်တော့လဲ
why?	ba-hpyi'-lọ-le:	ဘာဖြစ်လို့လဲ။
how much?	be-lau'-le:	ဘယ်လောက်လဲ
who?	be-dhu	ဘယ်သူ
whose?	be-dhụ-ha-le:	ဘယ်သူ့ဟာလဲ။
What do you want to do?	ba lo'-chin-le:?	ဘာ လုပ်ချင်လဲ။

Where's the bathroom?	ein-dha be-hma-le:?	အိမ်သာ ဘယ်မှာလဲ။
market	zei:	ဈေး
hotel	ho-te	ဟိုတယ်
hospital	hsei:-yon	ဆေးရုံ
airport	lei-zei'	လေဆိပ်
embassy	than-yon:	သံရုံး
this	da	ဒါ
that	e:-da	အဲဒါ
here	di-hma	ဒီမှာ
there	e:-di-hma	အဲဒီမှာ
over there	ho-hma	ဟိုမှာ
Whats this?	da-ba-le:?	ဒါဘာလဲ
What's that?	e:-da ba-le:?	အဲဒါ ဘာလဲ။
Whose is this?	da be-dhụ-ha-le:	ဒါ ဘယ်သူ့ဟာလဲ။
hello? (on the phone)	he:-lo	ဟဲလို
Is John home?	jɔn ein-hma-la:?	ဂျွန် အိမ်မှာလား။
I'd like to speak with John.	jɔn-nẹ pyɔ:-ɟin-de.	ဂျွန်နဲ့ ပြောချင်တယ်။
John is not home.	jɔn ein-hma mə-shị-bu:	ဂျွန် အိမ်မှာ မရှိဘူး။
really	də-ge	တကယ်
right?	-nɔ?	နော်
if	yin	ရင်
because	-lọ	လို့
not yet...	mə-...-thei:-bu:	မ...သေးဘူး။

[I'm] finished already.	pi:-thwa:-bi	ပြီးသွားပြီ။
but	da-bei-mẹ	ဒါပေမဲ့
didn't, don't	mə-...-bu:	မ...ဘူး
Don't do that.	da mə-lo'-nẹ	ဒါ မလုပ်နဲ့။
Don't go.	mə-thwa:-nẹ	မသွားနဲ့။
please	-pa/ba (particle)	ပါ
What is your name?	na-me be-lo-hkɔ-le:	နာမည် ဘယ်လိုခေါ်လဲ။
[My] name is john.	na-me jɔn-ba	နာမည် ဂျွန်ပါ။
What kind of work do you do?	ba lo'-thə-le:?	ဘာ လုပ်သလဲ။
I'm a doctor.	hsə-ya-wun-ba.	ဆရာဝန်ပါ။
lawyer	shẹi-nei	ရှေ့နေ
soldier	si'-tha:	စစ်သား
student (m)	jaun:-dha:	ကျောင်းသား
student (f)	jaun:-dhu	ကျောင်းသူ
professor	pa-mau'-hkạ	ပါမောက္ခ
engineer	in-ɟin-ni-ya	အင်ဂျင်နီယာ
tourist	tu:-ri'	တူးရစ်
monk	hpon:-ɟi:	ဘုန်းကြီး
Where are you from?	be-gạ-la-dhə-le:?	ဘယ်ကလာသလဲ။
I'm from America.	ə-mei-ri-kạ-gạ-ba.	အမေရိကကပါ။
Japan	ɟə-pan	ဂျပန်
China	tə-yo'	တရုတ်
India	ein-dị-yạ	အိန္ဒိယ
Thailand	htain:	ထိုင်း

England	in-gə-lan	အင်္ဂလန်
Do you like Myanmar?	myan-ma-pye-go jai'-la:?	မြန်မာပြည်ကို ကြိုက်လား။
Myanmar people are very nice.	myan-ma-lu-myo: -dwei thei' kaun:-de.	မြန်မာလူမျိုးတွေ သိပ် ကောင်းတယ်။
Yangon is very hot.	yan-gon thei' pu-de.	ရန်ကုန် သိပ် ပူတယ်။
Myanmar is beautiful.	myan-ma-nain-gan hla̱-de.	မြန်မာနိုင်ငံ လှတယ်။
It rains a lot.	mo: ə-yan: yua-de.	မိုး အရမ်း ရွာတယ်။
I like Yangon.	yan-gon-go jai'-te.	ရန်ကုန်ကို ကြိုက်တယ်။
Can you speak Burmese?	bə-ma-zə-ga: pyɔ: -da'-la:?	ဗမာစကား ပြောတတ်လား။
Can you speak English?	in:-gə-lei'-sə-ga: pyɔ: -da'-la:?	အင်္ဂလိပ်စကား ပြောတတ်လား။
I want to speak Burmese.	bə-ma-zə-ga: pyɔ: -ɟin-de.	ဗမာစကား ပြောချင်တယ်။
Please speak slowly.	hpyei:-byei: pyɔ:-ba.	ဖြေးဖြေး ပြောပါ။
Please say that again.	hta' pyɔ:-ba.	ထပ် ပြောပါ။
Can you write in Myanmar?	myan-ma-za yei:-da' -thə-la:	မြန်မာစာ ရေးတတ်သလား။
I can write a little bit.	ne:-ne: yei:-da'-te	နည်းနည်း ရေးတတ်တယ်။
I don't understand (polite form).	na-mə-le-ba-bu:	နားမလည်ပါဘူး
I can't hear.	mə-ja:-ya̱-bu:	မကြားရဘူး။
I am studying	bə-ma-zə-ga:	ဗမာစကား

Burmese.	thin-nei-de	သင်နေတယ်။
I'm learning Burmese from this book.	di sa-o'-kạ bə-ma-lo thin-nei-de	ဒီစာအုပ်က ဗမာလို သင်နေတယ်။
What do you call this in Burmese?	bə-ma-lo be-lo hkɔ-dhə-le:?	ဗမာလို ဘယ်လို ခေါ်သလဲ။
What does __ mean?	... ə-de-pe ba-le:?	...အဓိပ္ပာယ် ဘာလဲ။
How old are you?	ə-the' be-lau'-le:	အသက် ဘယ်လောက်လဲ။
I'm thirty years old.	ə-the' thon:-ze ba.	အသက် သုံးဆယ်ပါ။
Where do you live?	be-hma nei-dhə-le:?	ဘယ်မှာ နေသလဲ။
I live at (in) _____ .	...nei-de	...နေတယ်
How many brothers & sisters do you have?	maun-hnə-mạ be-hne-yau' shị-dhə-le:?	မောင်နှမ ဘယ်နှစ်ယောက် ရှိသလဲ။
Are you married?	ein-daun shị-dhə-la:?	အိမ်ထောင် ရှိသလား။
I'm married.	ein-daun-jạ-pi:-bi	အိမ်ထောင် ကျပြီးပြီ။
I'm single.	lu-lu'-pa.	လူလွတ်ပါ။
I'm divorced.	tə-hkụ-la'-pa.	တခုလပ်ပါ။
My wife passed away.	zə-ni: thei-thwa:-bi.	ဇနီး သေသွားပြီ။
How is the weather?	ya-dhi-u-tu be-lo-le:?	ရာသီဥတုဘယ်လိုလဲ။
It's hot.	pu-de.	ပူတယ်။
It's cold.	ei:-de.	အေးတယ်။
Can [I] see you tomorrow?	mə-ne'-hpyan tweị-nain-mə-la:?	မနက်ဖြန် တွေ့နိုင်မလား။

Can you teach me Myanmar?	myan-ma-lo thin-bei:-mə-la:?	မြန်မာလို သင်ပေးမလား။
I like (it).	jai'-te.	ကြိုက်တယ်။
I don't like (it).	mə-jai'-hpu:.	မကြိုက်ဘူး။
I like Myanmar people.	myan-ma-lu-myo: -dwei-go jai'-te.	မြန်မာလူမျိုးတွေကို ကြိုက်တယ်။
[You] are kind.	jin-na-de.	ကြင်နာတယ်။
Where are you staying?	be-hma te:-dhə-le:?	ဘယ်မှာတည်းသလဲ။
I am staying at the Kandawgyi hotel.	kan-dɔ-ji: ho' -te-hma ba.	ကန်တော်ကြီး ဟိုတယ်မှာပါ။
Here is my address.	da jə-mạ lei'-sa.	ဒါ ကျွန်မ လိပ်စာ။
Here is my phone number.	da jə-mạ hpon: -nan-ba'	ဒါ ကျွန်မ ဖုန်းနံပါတ်။
Can I have your address?	lei'-sa pei:-ba.	လိပ်စာ ပေးပါ။
Can I have your phone number?	hpon:-nan-ba' pei:-ba.	ဖုန်းနံပါတ် ပေးပါ။
Give me a call.	hpon:-hse'-nɔ.	ဖုန်းဆက်နော်။
Can I call you?	hpon:-hkɔ-lọ yạ-mə-la:	ဖုန်းခေါ်လို့ ရမလား။
I'll leave tomorrow.	mə-ne'-hpyan htwe'-me.	မနက်ဖြန် ထွက်မယ်။
I will go back next week.	nau'-ə-pa' pyan-me.	နောက်အပတ် ပြန်မယ်။

In a Restaurant

I want to order ...	...hma-me-nɔ.	...မှာမယ်နော်॥
What would you like to eat?	ba sa:-ʝin-dhə-le:.	ဘာ စားချင်သလဲ॥
What would you like to drink?	ba thau'-chin-dhə-le:?	ဘာ သောက်ချင်သလဲ॥
Bring water, please.	yei pei:-ba.	ရေ ပေးပါ॥
I'd like a serving of fried rice.	htə-min:-ʝɔ tə-bwe: lo-ʝin-de.	ထမင်းကြော် တစ်ပွဲ လိုချင်တယ်॥
I'd like some more rice.	htə-min:-hta' lo-ʝin-de.	ထမင်းထပ် လိုချင်တယ်॥
I'd like some ice.	yei-ge: lo-ʝin-de.	ရေခဲ လိုချင်တယ်॥
Is it spicy?	sa'-thə-la:?	စပ်သလား॥
Is it too spicy?	ə-yan: sa'-thə-la:?	အရမ်း စပ်သလား॥
It's very spicy.	ə-yan: sa'-te.	အရမ်း စပ်တယ်॥
It's not spicy.	mə-sa'-hpu:	မစပ်ဘူး॥
Does it taste good?	kaun:-la:?	ကောင်းလား॥
It tastes good.	sa:-kaun:-de.	စားကောင်းတယ်॥
It doesn't taste good.	sa:-mə-kaun:-bu:	စားမကောင်းဘူး॥
It's delicious.	ə-yạ-dha shị-de	အရသာ ရှိတယ်॥
food	ə-sa:-ə-sa	အစားအစာ
Myanmar food	myan-ma-ə-sa:-ə-sa	မြန်မာအစားအစာ
I want to eat	myan-ma-ə-sa:-	မြန်မာအစားအစာ

Myanmar food.	ə-sa sa:-ɟin-de.	စားချင်တယ်॥
dessert	ə-cho-bwe:	အချိုပွဲ
I want dessert.	ə-cho-bwe: lo-ɟin-de	အချိုပွဲ လိုချင်တယ်॥
I'm full.	wạ-bi.	ဝပြီ॥
That's enough	tɔ-bi	တော်ပြီ॥
I'm drunk.	mu:-de	မူးတယ်
alcohol	ə-ye'	အရက်
"check, [please]."	shin:-me.	ရှင်းမယ်॥
beef	a-me:	အမဲ
beer	bi-ya	ဘီယာ
boil/boiled	pyo'	ပြုတ်
chicken	je'	ကြက်
coffee	kɔ-hpi	ကော်ဖီ
crab	gə-nan:	ဂဏန်း
curry	hin:	ဟင်း
duck	be:	ဘဲ
eat	sa:-de	စားတယ်
chicken egg	je'-u	ကြက်ဥ
noodles	hkau'-hswe:	ခေါက်ဆွဲ
fish	nga:	ငါး
fry/fried	jɔ	ကြော်
fruit	thi'-thi:	သစ်သီး

grill/grilled	ken	ကင်
ice	yei-ge:	ရေခဲ
milk	nọ	နို့
pork	we'	ဝက်
cooked rice	htə-min:	ထမင်း
seafood	pin-le-za	ပင်လယ်စာ
shrimp	bə-zun	ပုစွန်
soup	hin:-jo	ဟင်းချို
black tea	la'-hpe'-ye	လက်ဖက်ရည်
oolong or plain tea	yei-nwe:-jan:, yei-nwe:	ရေနွေးကြမ်း၊ ရေနွေး
vegetable	hin:-dhi:-hin:-yue'	ဟင်းသီးဟင်းရွက်
vegetarian	the'-tha'-lu'	သက်သတ်လွတ်
water	yei	ရေ

Expressing Needs and Feelings

I'm hungry.	bai-hsa-de.	ဗိုက်ဆာတယ်။
I'm thirsty.	yei-nga'-te.	ရေငတ်တယ်။
I'm tired/exhausted.	mɔ:-de.	မောတယ်။
I'm sleepy.	ei'-chin-de.	အိပ်ချင်တယ်။
I'm happy.	pyɔ-de.	ပျော်တယ်။
I'm excited.	se'-hlo'-sha:-de.	စိတ်လှုပ်ရှားတယ်။

I'm hot.	pu-de.	ပူတယ်॥
I'm cold.	ei:-de.	အေးတယ်॥
I'm not well.	nei-mə-kaun:-bu:.	နေမကောင်းဘူး॥
I have a headache.	gaun: kai'-te.	ခေါင်း ကိုက်တယ်॥
I have a stomach ache.	bai'-na-de.	ဗိုက်နာတယ်॥
I need some medicine.	hsei:-thau'-hpọ-lo'-de.	ဆေးသောက်ဖို့လိုတယ်॥
I need some sleep.	ei' pyɔ-bọ lo-de.	အိပ်ပျော်ဖို့လိုတယ်॥
I want to see a doctor.	hsə-ya-wun pyạ-jin-de.	ဆရာဝန် ပြချင်တယ်॥
Come here!	di-go la!	ဒီကို လာ॥
Help!	ku-nyi-ba!	ကူညီပါ॥
Watch out!	thə-dị!	သတိ॥
I want to drink some water.	yei thau'-chin-de.	ရေ သောက်ချင်တယ်॥
I want to drink a glass of beer.	bi-ya tə-hkwe' thau'-jin-de.	ဘီယာ တစ်ခွက် သောက်ချင်တယ်॥
I want to buy some medicine.	hsei: we-jin-de.	ဆေးဝယ်ချင်တယ်॥
I want to go to the restroom.	ein-dha thwa:-jin-de.	အိမ်သာ သွားချင်တယ်॥
It's too loud.	ə-yan: jei-ta-be:.	အရမ်း ကျယ်တာပဲ॥
Can you turn down the air conditioning?	e:-kon: pei'-pei:.	အဲကွန်း ပိတ်ပေး॥
Can you turn up the air conditioning?	e:-kon: hpwiṇ-bei:.	အဲကွန်း ဖွင့်ပေး॥

Can you turn on the fan?	pan-ka hpwiṇ-bei:.	ပန်ကာ ဖွင့်ပေး။
May I use the phone?	te-li-hpon: thon:-lọ yạ-mə-la:?	တယ်လီဖုန်း သုံးလို့ ရမလား။
May I have some water?	yei thau'-lọ yạ-mə-la:?	ရေ သောက်လို့ ရမလား။
I'm lost.	lan: pyau'-nei-de.	လမ်း ပျောက်နေတယ်။
How do I get to ___?	...be-lo thwa:-mə-le:?	...ဘယ်လို သွားမလဲ။
I need more money.	pai'-hsan hta'-lo-de	ပိုက်ဆံ ထပ်လိုတယ်။
I need to change money.	ngwei-le:-bọ-lo-de.	ငွေလဲဖို့လိုတယ်။
I want to go back [home].	ein pyan-jin-de.	အိမ် ပြန်ချင်တယ်။
I want to ___ (verb).	...chin/jin-de.	...ချင်တယ်။
I understand.	na:-le-de.	နားလည်တယ်။
I don't understand.	na-mə-le-bu:.	နားမလည်ဘူး။
I don't know.	mə-thị-bu:.	မသိဘူး။
I believe (you).	yon-de.	ယုံတယ်။
I'm sure.	thei-ja-de.	သေချာတယ်။
I'm not sure.	mə-thei-ja-bu:.	မသေချာဘူး။
I'm joking.	yi-zə-ya pyɔ:-de.	ရယ်စရာ ပြောတယ်။
I agree.	thə-bɔ:-tu-de.	သဘောတူတယ်။
No problem.	kei'-sa mə-shi-bu:.	ကိစ္စမရှိဘူး။

a little bit	ne:-ne:	နည်းနည်း
I forgot.	mei̯-dhwa:-bi.	မေ့သွားပြီ။
I don't remember.	thə-di̯-mə-ya̯-bu:.	သတိမရဘူး။
Let's go.	thwa:-zo̯	သွားစို့။
I'm busy.	ə-lo'-sho'-te.	အလုပ်ရှုပ်တယ်။
I'm sad.	wun:-ne:-de.	ဝမ်းနည်းတယ်။
I'm angry.	sei'-hso:-de.	စိတ်ဆိုးတယ်။
I'm homesick.	ein-go lwan:-de.	အိမ်ကိုလွမ်းတယ်။
I'm confused.	sho'-te.	ရှုပ်တယ်။
I'm embarrassed.	ə-she'-kwe:-de.	အရှက်ကွဲတယ်။
I'm bored.	ngi:-ngwe̯-de.	ငြီးငွေ့တယ်။
I'm worried.	sei'-pu-de.	စိတ်ပူတယ်။
I'm scared.	jau'-te.	ကြောက်တယ်။
I'm heartbroken.	ə-the:-gwe:-de	အသည်းကွဲတယ်။
No smoking.	hsei:-lei' mə-thau'-ya̯	ဆေးလိပ် မသောက်ရ။
Speak up.	pyɔ:-ba.	ပြောပါ။
I made a mistake.	hma:-dhwa:-de.	မှားသွားတယ်။
Please wait a moment.	hkə-na̯ saun̯-ba.	ခဏ စောင့်ပါ။
Good luck.	kan-kaun:-ba-zei	ကံကောင်းပါစေ။
I wish you happiness.	pyɔ-shwin-ba-zei.	ပျော်ရွှင်ပါစေ။

Index

About the Author

Gene Mesher holds a Ph.D. in Management Information Systems from the University of Arizona, a M.S. in Biology from the University of Michigan and a Master's of Science in Engineering from the University of Washington. He is a former Fulbright scholar and retired professor of Information Systems at California State University. He has travelled to Southeast Asia for the last 15 years, studying telecommunications markets in Malaysia, Singapore, Thailand and other parts of Asia. Dr. Mesher has authored of more than 50 articles and reports on telecommunications and information technologies most of which have covered developments in Asian countries. His interest in language-learning is long-standing and he has studied many languages including French, Spanish, Portuguese, Japanese, Malay, Persian and Thai.